PRAISE FOR *The Lost Choice*

"Bottom line, I'm a better person for having experienced Andy Andrews' incredible storytelling talent. For the special people in your life, there could be no better gift."

—BILL AMES, Executive, General Motors

"The story of *The Lost Choice* is the best I've read in years, but the book's message will land it on the desks of the world's business leaders. This is a masterpiece—a thrilling mystery that can change your life. Do yourself a huge favor and read this book. I loved it."

—DON BRINDLEY, Former President, Merrill Lynch Insurance

"Andy Andrews weaves the golden threads of love, truth, and wisdom into a brilliant tapestry of a story."

—DELILAH, Nighttime Radio Personality

"*The Lost Choice* is a spectacular novel that will change your business . . . and your life. Og Mandino's passion was storytelling that made a difference. He has passed the baton to Andy Andrews and the tradition continues!"

—TODD DUNCAN, Author of *High Trust Selling* & *Killing the Sale*

"*The Lost Choice* is a masterpiece of ideas and emotions—a magnificent and bold achievement that will be an inspiration to all who read it."

—DEBBIE ELLIOTT, National Public Radio

"Andy Andrews knows about success—and in *The Lost Choice* he deftly, yet subtly delivers a powerful message of success to the reader. A lesson for life."

—GENERAL ROBERT H. "DOC" FOGLESONG, USAF

"A true treasure—another inspiring tale from one of this century's greatest storytellers."

—SCOTT JEFFREY, Author of *Journey to the Impossible*

"*The Lost Choice* is told so simply by author Andy Andrews. The special effect of this book is pure genius. It is a story for generations."

—JOSEPH G. LAKE, Cofounder, Children's Miracle Network

"*The Lost Choice* will impact the personal and financial lives of every business person who reads it. I have personally made Andy Andrews' books required reading for everyone in our company. It is a book you definitely need to pass on to your friends."

—JIM PACE, President and CEO, Group VI Corporation

"Andy Andrews has done it yet again! Just like with *The Traveler's Gift* he had me from the first page! Andy is a man with a message you must hear and apply to your life . . . Awesome!!!!"

—DAVE RAMSEY, Radio Host and Author of the *New York Times* best-seller *The Total Money Makeover*

"You think there are no second chances in life? Andy Andrews will prove you wrong. Trust me—read this book. *The Lost Choice* blew me away."

—TODD RAINSBERGER, Producer, ESPN

"Andy Andrews is a new breed of novelist—one who makes 'chronological discoveries' an art form. This is a beautiful story that will keep you guessing until the last page."

—JOHN R. SCHNEIDER, Actor and Recording Artist

"Andy Andrews has become one of the largest influences in my life. If I could choose one gift to give every person with whom I cross paths, it would be this book."

—CHRIS SMITH, Executive, Coca-Cola Enterprises

"*The Lost Choice* represents the definition of a class act. As Andy's latest triumph, the book owes both its significance and success to the way it seamlessly unites critical life elements."

—ZACHARY SMITH, President, Delphian Internet

"Once again Andy Andrews has created a masterpiece. *The Lost Choice* confirms the promise passed from generation to generation, that through our choices we, too, can attain greatness and make our mark in history."

—DEANNIA C. SMITH, English Teacher,
Oxford High School, Oxford, Alabama

"Another masterpiece by Andy Andrews with a dramatic storyline, great writing, historical value, a plot that captivates our minds and provides an escape from the present by sending us on another exhilarating adventure. As a congressman, my time is very limited. *The Lost Choice* joins *The Traveler's Gift* as time well spent."

—CONGRESSMAN ZACH WAMP, Tennessee, Third Congressional District

"I am Andy's #1 fan. I have recommended Andy's book to every person in our organization. Andy's values of leadership, collaboration, and responsibility are reflected in our company culture."

—MARK WILLIS, President, Keller Williams Realty International

THE LOST CHOICE

CHOICE

A Legend *of* Personal Discovery

ANDY ANDREWS

THOMAS NELSON
Since 1798

NASHVILLE   DALLAS   MEXICO CITY   RIO DE JANEIRO

CONTACT ANDY

Book Andy for your corporate event:
(800) 726-ANDY (2639)

Learn more at
www.AndyAndrews.com

Published in Nashville, Tennessee. Thomas Nelson is a trademark of Thomas Nelson, Inc.

Library of Congress Cataloging-in-Publication Data

Andrews, Andy, 1959–
  The lost choice : a legend of personal discovery / Andy Andrews.
    p. cm.
  Includes bibliographical references.
  ISBN 13: 978-0-7852-6139-1 (hardcover)
  1. Conduct of life. 2. Success. I. Title.
  BJ1597.A52 2004
  813'.54—dc22   2004003469

Printed in the United States of America
10 11 12 13 QG 13 12 11 10

Dedicated to Sandra K. Dorff, Paula Tebbe, and Susie White—three ladies whose choices have had a profound effect on my family and me. Thanks, SB, PC, and Woowie!

No individual has any right to come into this world and go out of it without leaving behind him distinct and legitimate reasons for having passed through it.

—GEORGE WASHINGTON CARVER

⚔ PROLOGUE

KASIMIR SHIELDED HIS EYES WITH BOTH HANDS as he peered intently into the sun's last rays. Another tear made a track through the dust on his browned face and fell from his chin. His age was eleven summers now, almost a man, and his father's falcon was missing.

Alem, his father, had often made it clear that he was not yet ready to command the valuable huntress. The falcon had been a gift from a prince, given to Alem as a sign of respect. Her name was Skei—a word the prince had told them meant "swift." She was as tall as Kasimir's arm was long, and her talons completely enveloped the leather covering on his skinny shoulder where she sometimes sat as Kasimir rode his father's camel. Skei was snow white with jet-black slashes in her feathers, and she wore a hood that matched the jesses, long hide straps, on her legs.

Intending to prove his resourcefulness and maturity, the boy had impulsively released the bird earlier in the day when the shadows were small. Food was scarce, and the rabbit he

1

had glimpsed would have made an excellent meal. Unfortunately, the beautiful falcon had not seen fit to return with the rabbit or any rabbit or to return at all for that matter.

"Kasi!" The boy cringed at the sound of his father's voice. It was not an unkind voice for he was not an unkind man. It was, however, the voice of a man who demanded honesty. And Kasimir would be honest with him now. "Kasi!" Alem called again.

"Coming, Father!"

THE DESERT GLOWED WITH THE APPROACHING DUSK as the velvet sand returned its heat to the evening sky. For three days the Bedouins had rested at Elim. Fewer than fivescore—one hundred—men, women, and children comprised this nomadic group. Generally wandering an area between the Springs of Marah and the mountain they called Jabal al Lawz, these people did not count Alem and his son as part of their tribe. Neither, however, did they consider them intruders. Alem and Kasi had come and gone several times over the last four summers, each arrival bringing news of interest from Egypt, Midian, even Rome!

Their story was known to all. Alem's wife had died when Kasi was still a baby. He never took another woman, choosing instead to care for his boy alone and live a life "wandering among the wanderers." It was incredibly dangerous. There were slave traders, thieves, and, of course, the desert itself. Yet season after season the father and son traveled together, sometimes with one tribe or another, but most often alone.

Alem was regarded as very unique among the desert people, for two reasons. One, he had a gift of clarity. Many said that he could see through a head directly into a heart.

Alem was not a prophet or a religious leader and almost never addressed a gathering, but was often sought as a companion by the fire or as the caravan moved across the sand. He spoke directly, but with compassion, discerning one's past with an eye to guiding the future. Alem was an oracle of truth.

Second, it was widely known that Alem had a possession. Beyond one's camel, robes, and perhaps a weapon such as a sword or even a falcon or sight hound, this was almost unheard of. But Alem had one. A possession. And no one had any idea what it was.

ALEM'S POSSESSION WAS ROLLED THICKLY IN BURGUNDY linen and bound with cord cut from a black burnoose. A short leather strap wound tightly around Alem's left shoulder and neck, allowing the object to settle into the folds of his robe. Thus, it was carried next to his chest, where his eyes could watch the possession and his arms could protect it. Always and all the time.

Alem slept, ate, and traveled with the possession awkwardly attached to him. It was of an indeterminate size due to the bulky cloth in which it was wrapped, but "a bit smaller than the foot of a camel" had been accepted as the general dimension by those who engaged in endless discussions about this curiosity. It was whispered that even Kasimir, his boy, had never seen the item.

Kasi found his father seated alone, cross-legged beside a small fire, one of many burning throughout the palms. "Ahh! There you are, my son," Alem said as the boy entered the firelight.

"Father, I have something to tell you," he began right away.

"And I am anxious to hear your news," Alem said with a

smile. "But first, be seated and partake of today's abundance, for soon today will be gone. Eat!"

"Father, what I have to say—"

"Will wait until you have eaten. Sit, my son." He gestured toward the ground to his right and as Kasi sat beside him, Alem continued. "We will depart this evening. Are you hungry?"

"Yes, Father."

"Then eat." Alem pulled a stick from over the fire and removed the leg of what appeared to be a large roasted hare. He brushed a cinder from the meat with his free hand, passed it to Kasi, and said, "A small band of us—perhaps half a score—will move north when the fires are low. Will you halter Biba when you are through here? She is with the group of camels under the fig tree."

"As you wish, Father. But first, I must tell you—"

"Kasi!"

"Yes, Father?"

"Eat."

"Yes, Father."

Kasimir took a big bite and chewed thoughtfully as he studied the man everyone said he so closely resembled. His father's black hair barely showed around the edges of what was once a white burnoose. His skin was dark, burned to an even shade by the sun and the wind, and it contrasted sharply with his even, white teeth. His nose was long and straight, perfect except for the small scar running across the bridge, and his chin was strong. One could easily see Alem's chin, for his beard had never grown. More stubble than beard, the whiskers were short and thinly spaced.

The boy smiled at his father as he took another bite. *No one looks at his beard anyway,* he thought. *They only see his eyes!* It was true. Alem's eyes were bright blue. As rare as diamonds, Kasi had heard the women say. He had seen men avert their own eyes when they met his father. *Blue eyes,* Kasi mused. *Blue eyes like azure. And I have them too.*

Suddenly Kasi frowned. "Is this rabbit, Father?" He held up a bone from which he had eaten the meat.

"Rabbit . . . hare. Yes." Alem's eyebrows lifted.

"From where did we receive such a blessing?"

"Well, let me see." Alem rubbed his finger alongside his nose. "Could it have been a gift from another family?"

"No, Father. There has not been enough to eat, much less to share!"

"Yes, I see what you mean," Alem said smiling. "No, it would not have been a gift. And we know what the dogs do if they catch one—no sharing there. Do you suppose perhaps Biba ran this one down?"

Kasi laughed. He was being teased and he knew it. "No, Father! I don't believe our grouchy old camel caught a rabbit! But I have never seen you run fast enough to catch one either!"

"That is very true, my son. I am not as fleet as the hare." Alem quickly put his arm around Kasi and lay straight back, pulling the boy with him until both were side by side, flat on their backs, looking upward. He pointed with the bone in his hand, directing his son's gaze to a palm branch above them. "No, I am not as fast as a rabbit, but I do enjoy its taste. And that is why I take care of my falcon!"

"Skei!" Kasi exclaimed. The beautiful bird sat above them, cocking her head curiously. Turning, he asked, "Where did you find her? I was about to tell you she was lost and that it was all my fault."

"She found me, Kasi, with the rabbit, only moments after

you let her go." Alem narrowed his eyes a bit and smiled. "And while yet another conversation remains about you and Skei, I must admit pride that you were willing to accept responsibility for the disobedient choice you made. That is evidence of a growing character."

Kasi rolled over and moved into a sitting position as Alem stood and began wrapping the folds of his burnoose around his left arm. "I want to do what is right," the boy said, "but sometimes I want to do what I . . ." He paused and furrowed his brow. Then, looking up at his father again, he stumbled ahead. "Well, I suppose sometimes I want to do what I want to do. Is that evidence of bad character?"

Alem smiled at Kasi and extended his arm toward the falcon. "Your character is your essence; it is what you are. Your character is determined by the choices you make when no one will ever know what you did . . . or didn't."

Skei dropped from the palm branch and landed heavily on Alem's arm. "You must build your character daily, my son. And immediately. All blossoms of tomorrow, and all weeds as well, are in the seeds you are sowing today. Your influence, your wealth, and ultimately your legacy will be decided by this one thing. For ultimately, no person can ever rise beyond the restrictions of his own character."

For a moment, the man and boy simply looked at each other. Blue eyes burning blue eyes into memory by firelight. Kasi spoke first. "I understand," he said.

"I knew you would," his father responded softly. Then, slipping into the shadows, he said, "Quickly now. Ready the camel."

THE DARKNESS WAS VAST AND COMPLETE; THE MOON-less night a flowing tide of ebony muslin drawn like a tent over the tiny caravan. Eight camels plodded in a loosely defined single file gradually gaining ground in the general direction of Polaris, the brightest of the stars shredding this blackest of nights. The soft voices of the Bedouins drifted across the sand and emptied into nothingness.

Biba was the third camel. She was draped in red silk and carried two immense baskets—one on either side of her hump—heavily loaded with the spices cardamom, cassia, black cumin, as well as more red silk. Seated on the center of Biba's hump, hands on the reins, a foot resting on each basket, was Alem with Skei the falcon, asleep, perched on his shoulder. Kasi snuggled in close, sitting practically in Alem's lap, his father's arms draped around his shoulders. They swayed in an awkward unison to the camel's gait.

In the starlight, Kasi could see the other men and their desert steeds in front of and behind them. They were headed to Colonia Aelia, the Emperor Hadrian's new city. There they would spend a few days in the spice market. After trading for food and the essentials of life, the Bedouins would make their way back across the Desert of Shur to rejoin their people near Marah. Alem and Kasi would not make the return trip.

"Why must we leave these people, Father?" Kasi asked quietly.

"For us, my son, there is only safety in movement," came the answer. "And then, only a measure. You are aware that there are those who seek us for want of the possession." Alem absently touched the rolled-up object that was tied to his chest. "And these are simply violent times."

"If someone tried to hurt us," Kasi said shaking his fist, "I would think of many ways to hurt them in return!"

Alem laughed gently. "Those thoughts would take too much of your precious time, I fear. Time spent getting even would be better used gaining an understanding of yourself. Revenge is like biting a camel because the camel has bitten you. When you seek to get even, you are apt to do strange things!"

"Why do you say that I must understand myself?" Kasi puzzled. "I am quite certain that I already understand myself."

"Really?" Alem said as he leaned out and around his son's shoulder to see his face. Skei flapped her wings once, disturbed by the sudden movement. "Really, you do?"

"I think so," Kasi said, now not so certain.

"Then can you explain to me, my son, why you released Skei this morning when you clearly knew this was against my wishes? You knew it was wrong, yet you proceeded. Was it your desire to do evil?"

"No, Father," the boy stammered. "I was—"

"Were you intending to lose the bird?"

"No."

"Did you remember your father and his rule as you set Skei to flight?"

"Of course not!" Kasi declared. "I would never have done such a thing had I remembered your rule!"

Alem was quiet.

"That is not true," Kasi finally said. "I did remember your rule. I remembered your rule, and I did it anyway. And I don't know why. I am now quite certain that I do not understand myself."

Alem chuckled and gave the boy a hug. "You are only eleven summers, my son. There are grown men who struggle mightily with this concept. The result you are seeking is not mere understanding, but control. It is not enough to recognize what is right and true. One must control the impulse to do what is wrong and easy. Nothing will withstand a person who can conquer himself."

For a long time they rode without talking. Kasi thought about all his father had told him. He listened to Biba. Her feet made a squishing noise as they stepped through the sand and her breathing contained a small whistle. He could smell the saltiness of his father mingled with the mellow aroma of the cardamom and the sweetness of the cassia. And occasionally, he caught a whiff of Biba.

Alem moved his head forward and whispered in his son's ear. "Kasi?"

"Yes, Father," came the soft reply.

"Where are your thoughts leading you?"

"To your possession, Father. Will you tell me what it is?"

Alem was silent at first. When he spoke, he did so carefully in a voice just above a whisper. "It is an object of fear and an object of promise. An object of ridicule and of power. The possession displays abject poverty and incredible wealth. It contains death and birth and blindness and sight. And one day, it will be yours to protect."

Kasi shifted his weight as he took all this in. "If you won't tell me what it is, then what does it do?"

"I told you exactly what it is. As for what it does? It does nothing. It does, however, represent the power to do everything. It is believed and doubted, contemplated and ignored, pursued and avoided. Men will kill for it . . . and I would die to protect it."

"Where did you get it?"

"From my father many years ago." Alem cleared his throat. "He was entrusted with the possession and kept it hidden for many years. It was the only thing he left me, and it will be the only thing I am able to leave you, Kasi. It is a gift from a father to his son."

Kasi was more confused than ever. "Father," he questioned,

"why do we have to keep the object hidden? And if we can't use it, what good is it anyway?"

"Pay close attention, my son," Alem began. "There will come a time when the possession will be revealed to all. On that day, everything will change. Kingdoms will rise and fall . . . in a day! You must know that there are men who would die to make this happen and men who would die to prevent it from happening.

"The possession itself—the object—will never, alone, do anything. Even as you gain full knowledge of its history and destiny, it will do nothing but remain tied to your body. Kasi . . . turn around. I want to look at you." Alem picked up his son by the arms and helped him turn completely around—he was riding backward, but facing his father.

"My son," Alem said as he placed his hands on Kasi's shoulders and stared intently into his eyes, "an article of wood or metal or glass can achieve nothing. Set on a mantel in a fine home or on a mountaintop for all to see, it will never, by itself, plow a field or tend a sick person or cook a meal. An object can inspire, arouse, prove, encourage, justify, and confirm. But it can never produce.

"It is only by your hand that the mind's choices bear fruit. Intentions are like physical beauty—they mean nothing. At some point, a person must actually *do* something. One's beliefs must become works. By your hand, you establish evidence for others in the truth of what you believe."

Suddenly Biba violently threw her head to the side and stumbled to her knees. A scream from the end of the caravan pierced the calm night as the sand behind and in front of the Bedouins erupted with men brandishing swords, shooting bows, and shrieking at the top of their voices!

Biba slowly rolled over on her side, an arrow through

her neck, as Alem released Skei and swept Kasi from the dying camel. "Slavers, Kasi!" he yelled. "Roman slavers! Dig a hole under Biba! Quickly!"

As chaos raged around them in the darkness, Alem and Kasi hurriedly dug a trench in the sand alongside and under the camel. Men were running, swords were flashing and the boy heard the whistling rush of arrows being loosed as he looked up to see a man surrender. His father pushed him into the hole and said, "Dig in! Hide!"

On his knees behind the dead camel and the scattered baskets, Alem drew a sword from the folds of his burnoose. With a rapid jerk, he cut the bundle from his chest, sliced the cord binding it, and rolled the possession fully exposed onto the ground. It came to rest mere inches from Kasi's face. Despite the bedlam raging around him, the boy's eyes opened wide and his jaw dropped. Then his father took the sword and hacked it to pieces.

In three swift strokes, Alem severed the object into four parts. Horrified, Kasi yelled, "You destroyed it!" and started to scramble out of his hole.

Alem grabbed him and shoved him roughly back in. "Stay down, Kasi! The possession can never be destroyed! Everything I have told you will come to pass, but the time is not now. These men must not find it here! Take this," he said and placed a piece of the possession in Kasi's hand. "I love you, my son!" And with those words, Alem grabbed the dead camel and with a desperate effort pulled the animal completely over his boy.

Uncomfortable and terror-stricken, Kasi lay still, barely able to breathe, listening to the fighting just above him. And just as suddenly as it had begun—it was over—quiet except for the barked commands of someone whose language he did not understand. He heard them moving off into the distance. Then silence. The entire attack had taken less than three minutes.

For a long time Kasi lay there. He was unsure of what to do. Finally, dizzy from the heat and lack of oxygen, the boy dug himself out. It wasn't easy, but by displacing sand and inching his arm out first, he was able to escape the hiding place that had saved him from . . . what?

Kasi stood up and looked around. The sun was rising in the eastern sky. He saw two more camels dead. And four human bodies, stripped of their robes, lying facedown in the sand. Fearfully, the boy crept over to the dead men. Glancing around, he knelt beside them. Three of the men, he saw, had long, full beards, but the fourth . . . he crawled over and turned the head.

It was not Alem.

Kasi stood up. So his father was not dead. Had he escaped? Was he captured? He heard a movement behind him and, startled, wheeled around to face it. Skei, he saw, had returned, landing on the back of her old friend Biba. Kasi looked at his fist, still tightly closed, and slowly opened it. A piece of the possession. A gift from a father to a son.

Near the dead camel, he saw that the other pieces of the possession were gone, but he found a shredded remnant of the burgundy linen and rolled it carefully around the piece that remained, tying it with black cord. Using a short strap of leather from Biba's halter, he wound it around his left shoulder and neck, then secured it to his chest where his eyes could watch it and his arms protect it. Always and all the time.

Kasi walked over to the falcon and rummaged around for a scrap of leather. Laying it across his shoulder, he allowed Skei to settle there for a moment. Examining the sunrise, the boy placed the warm rays to his right and strode purposefully to the north.

⚜ ONE

IT WAS SATURDAY MORNING, SUNNY AND WARM, a perfect June day in Colorado. As Mark Chandler walked into the den, he yawned and looked at his wife who was sitting in the recliner.

Dorry Chandler was the kind of woman people stared at, trying to determine if they thought she was attractive. She was five feet four inches tall if she stood on her tiptoes to be measured, which she was apt to do, and weighed an even one hundred pounds. Her red hair was accented by a sprinkling of freckles on her face. Mark walked over and kissed his wife on the top of her head.

"What time did you get in?"

"Late—eleven-thirty. Plane was delayed out of Dallas."

"Sorry I didn't wait up," Mark said as he sat on the arm of the chair. "Other than the late flight, was the trip okay?"

"Yeah, you know," Dorry shrugged. "Did the interview. In and out. No big deal."

"Do you have to go to the office today?" he asked.

13

"Nope. Wrote the article flying in and e-mailed it to the office last night while you snored." She messed up his hair and headed for the kitchen. "Coffee?" she asked.

"Sure, thanks," Mark said as he followed her in and sat down at the breakfast table. A Denver police officer in his fourteenth year, Mark was exactly two years older than his thirty-seven-year-old wife. He was average in height and build with dark, curly hair that occasionally grew over his ears. And that was okay. He was a detective sergeant and could get away with it.

The first day he had seen Dorry, she was arguing with his partner, who, at the time, was trying to give her a speeding ticket, and she was refusing to accept it. Standing at the rear of Dorry's beat-up white Buick LeSabre, Mark had been laughing so hard that his partner finally walked back to him and, fuming, handed him the ticket book. It had taken Mark about five more minutes to calm Dorry down and convince her to sign the ticket, but that was all the time it took for Mark to fall in love.

It had taken Dorry a bit longer to admit she was attracted to a policeman. After all, she was a newspaper reporter and had spent a great portion of her adult life fostering deep reservations about authority. In any case, they were married less than a year later and had their only child, Michael, six years after that.

Now Mark asked his bride of eleven years a familiar question. "How many cups have you already had?"

"Sixty or seventy. But I've only been awake a couple of hours. Don't start."

Mark had a theory about his wife and her personality as it related to coffee consumption. Simply put, he believed that while others might exhibit type A tendencies or be labeled a "driver" or "choleric" or one of the other terms in current use, Dorry *was* caffeine. Mark teased about her constant liquid companion, but had long since decided he did not really want her to quit. She would be an entirely different person without it, and he was happy with the wife he had.

"Sheesh!" he said, noticing the clock on the stove. "It's ten o'clock already. Why'd you let me sleep so late?"

"I don't know," Dorry answered. "You seemed tired." She sat down across from him and slid his favorite mug over. "Anyway, Michael was up early and wanted to play with Jonathan." Jonathan was seven, the youngest of three children who belonged to their neighbors, Richard and Kendra Harper.

"Where are they now?" Mark asked. "Next door?"

Without moving the coffee cup or taking her eyes off Mark, Dorry smiled and slid her forefinger from the mug handle, pointing it out the big picture window. "In the ditch," she said.

Defining the boundary of the Chandler's backyard was a low area, a wet runoff that Mark proudly referred to as "the creek." Dorry called it a ditch.

Whatever it was, they couldn't keep their son out of it. Michael was a five-year-old with his mother's red hair and green eyes and his dad's personality. Interested in everything, he wanted to know where it came from, how it worked, *why* it worked, and quite often, what it looked like on the inside! Mark and Dorry had wanted more children, but after years of trying to conceive again, they had finally been told by several doctors that it was "an impossibility."

As Mark looked out the picture window, he saw the bobbing heads of two boys as they knelt, splashed, jumped, and scurried from one area to another. He chuckled and shook his head. "They'd probably roll around in that creek all day if we let 'em."

"Ditch," Dorry corrected. "Probably so." She stood and reached for another cup of coffee. "But we are going to the mall today, remember? Master Michael Chandler needs some summer clothes, and I could use a few things myself."

Mark groaned. "I forgot all about that, but yeah, I guess. We're still cooking out tonight with Richard and Kendra, right?"

"As far as I know. They said they would cook, so I'm not even thinking about it. You know their deal. When *we* cook, they bring nothing. Nothing! So tonight, guess what I'm bringing?"

"Nothing?" Mark asked innocently, trying not to laugh.

"That's exactly right," Dorry replied. "But I will bring an entire box of nothing."

A LITTLE LATER, AFTER HAVING BEEN CALLED THREE times by Mark, Dorry whistled once with her hands on her hips and their son tramped through the back door. "Let's go, buddy. Dad's in the shower. We're going to the mall. Are you dirty?"

"No, ma'am."

Dorry stuck her arm in front of him as he tried to squeeze by. "I didn't think you were, but I had to ask," she said. "I just couldn't see through all that mud covering up your cleanliness."

"Oh, Mom," Michael grinned, "don't be sarcasm."

Dorry stopped. With her eyes opened wide, she asked, "Where on earth did you learn *that* word?"

"Daddy. He said it was supposed to be your name. It's what Grampa wanted to make your name, but Nana wouldn't let him."

"Really?" Dorry stifled a laugh. "Remind me to tell you a story about Daddy later. Right now, we have to hustle. Take off your clothes here in the kitchen and run for the tub."

As the guys were bathing, Dorry poured another cup of coffee and started the washing machine. She turned the water temperature to its highest setting. *Forget color. It's all brown anyway,* she thought. Gathering up the clothes, Dorry noticed a heaviness to the blue jeans. Not surprised, she began to empty the pockets. It was something she had done for Mark ever since they'd been married, and now Michael was just like him. Mentally, she categorized the items, placing them on the counter by the sink or straight into the garbage can.

Whatever the heavy thing was, Dorry had to work the pocket inside out. Her hand barely fit into Michael's under-sized pockets anyway and this last item, certain to be the biggest rock yet, seemed truly stuck. Gradually, she was able to reverse the wet cotton fabric and remove . . . something.

It wasn't a rock, Dorry didn't think. But then again, maybe it was. She turned it over. It was metal. A bit smaller than her hand, crumpled into a vague rectangular shape, with some kind of small indentions all over it. Old looking, but not rusted. *Definitely metal,* she decided. *Unless it's a rock.*

IT WAS ALMOST A WEEK LATER WHEN DORRY REMEM-bered the "rock." She had put it in an empty flowerpot on the windowsill above the sink, intending to inspect it more closely when she wasn't in such a hurry.

Mark found it the following Thursday evening. They

always enjoyed the extra hour or so of daylight that summer provided and, most days, spent the time after work outdoors with Michael. From the patio where he and Michael were watching Dorry transplant clumps of daisies, Mark went inside to retrieve the pot.

A moment later, Mark unlocked and opened the window from the kitchen. "Is this the one you want?" he called, holding up the flowerpot.

Dorry glanced up. "Uh-huh. The yellow one."

Mark stepped through the door. "Do you want whatever this is *in* the pot?" he asked as he walked over. He shook the pot and made it rattle.

"What?" Dorry looked up.

"This thing." Mark reached into the pot and brought out the object. "Is this a throwaway?"

Recognition showed in Dorry's face as she straightened her back and removed her gardening gloves. "I forgot all about that," she said. "It was in Michael's pocket last week. I actually meant to show it to you."

"So don't throw it away?"

"Not yet. I want to look at it again. And we're ready to come in. The mosquitoes are killing us."

LATER THAT EVENING, THE FAMILY GATHERED IN THE den. "What do we want to talk about tonight?" Mark began. The television sat, rarely used, in the corner. Several years earlier Mark and Dorry had agreed that their jobs kept them current on as much news as they could stand, and neither wanted Michael to grow up with the television blaring constantly. So, unlike other families they knew, the Chandlers had developed a habit of talking.

"Hey, get that thing," Dorry said. "That thingie from the flowerpot. Where'd you put it?"

"Oh, yeah," Mark said as he got out of his recliner and headed for the kitchen. "Hang on." Seconds later, he returned with the object in his hand and a perplexed frown on his face.

"Come here and hold it where we can all see it," Dorry said as she made room on the couch. "Michael, you sit in Mama's lap."

Mark sat down and held the object at an angle to catch the light from the floor lamp. Reaching up to adjust the lampshade, he said, "Where did you say this came from?"

"From Monkey Boy's pocket," she answered and gave the child a quick tickle across the ribs. Michael giggled.

Mark looked at his son. "So where did *you* get it, Monkey Boy?"

"At the creek," Michael said.

"At the creek? Or *in* the creek?"

Michael looked thoughtful. There would come a time in his life, particularly as a teenager, when he would notice that the answers his parents required were to be delivered in excruciating detail. This was not Michael's fault—just a natural by-product of having a journalist for a mother and a detective for a father. But for now, he was only too happy to reply.

"It was kinda on the *side* of the creek."

Mark turned it over. "It's not a rock. It's too heavy. Kind of reddish brownish. It's hard. I can't nick it with my fingernail."

"Let me see it," Dorry said. Mark handed it to her. She held the edges up to the light. "See the cuts?" she said, pointing them out to her husband and son. "Sort of . . . indentions or something. It's like they have a pattern, but not really. It looks old, doesn't it?"

"Yep," Mark said as he stood up. "Old like me. And it's time to go to bed."

"Daddy, will you read me a story?"

Mark reached down and grabbed Michael, swinging him up into his arms. "Yes, I will, Monkey Boy!"

"Hang on a minute. I'm serious," Dorry said. "Don't you think this is old? I mean, really old?"

"Yeah, probably," Mark said as he turned the chortling five-year-old upside down.

"Yeah, probably?" Dorry imitated Mark's voice. "Yeah, probably? Do you not have any curiosity about this at all?"

Mark was tempted to answer her with a "yeah, probably," but instead said simply, "Look, Dorry, you have enough curiosity in you for all five of us, and there are only three in our family!"

"Well, I just would have thought . . ."

"Hey, if you really want to know, give it to Dylan and see what he can find out."

She scrunched up her face. "Who?"

"Dylan. Kendra's brother. You met him last Saturday night. He just moved here."

"Okay," she said as the recognition dawned on her face. "I remember. He's one of the new 'big dogs' at the museum, right?"

"In one department or another. Anyway, give it to him and see what he thinks."

"I think I will," Dorry answered and kissed Michael goodnight. "I'm sure we'll get along. I saw what he brought to his sister's cookout."

Mark paused, then chuckled as he caught the reference. "Nothing?"

"Yes," she smirked. "An entire box."

❧ TWO

THE GROUP OF MEN STOOD IN THE FACTORY courtyard shortly after midday. Their guide was the owner of Duetch Emailwaren Fabrik, a producer of enameled goods. Oberführer Eberhard Steinhauser was enjoying a tour of the grounds with his second, Unterscharführer Herman Bosche, several other officers, and an adjutant who had been assigned to the men for the morning.

Steinhauser and Bosche were resplendent in their uniforms. Black-on-black with ornamental silver and an occasional trace of red, the sharply tailored clothing had been created specially for officers of the Staatspolizei. On each shoulder of the jacket were the letters *SS* laid over a lightning bolt. Medals and ribbons for loyalty and bravery stood in contrast over the left breast, but the uniform's focal point was the cap—steeply arched in the front and centered with a silver skull and crossbones.

Their tour guide was also dressed expensively, but in a business suit. Navy blue, it was one of many double-breasted suits owned by the direktor of the company. A tall, thirty-four-year-old man, he wore his dark hair combed straight back, and though he smoked incessantly, he somehow managed to appear stately. The starched white shirt he wore provided an adequate background for the red and grey tie, but one's eye ran immediately to the lapel, not to the tie. There hung a large ornamental gold-on-black Hakenkreuz, a swastika, the symbol of a member in good standing of the Nazi Party.

Steinhauser spoke. "A pity we must leave, Herr Direktor. Your hospitality has been greatly appreciated, and I assure you, duly noted. You will not forget my poor mother?"

"No, no! Of course not," the direktor replied as he placed his hand on the oberführer's shoulder and gently started him moving toward the exit. "Should I deliver it to her personally, or would you have me direct it through her loving son?"

The small group laughed. "Just have it sent to my office. Five complete sets of your finest, mind you. I will take care of Mama." The group laughed again.

The direktor had lost count of how many mothers of officers had "lost their enamelware in bombings." It wasn't remotely true, of course. The entire charade was merely an unspoken business transaction. All parties knew that the enamelware would quickly find its way onto the black market, lining the pockets of the officers. It was a bribe, pure and simple.

Not a stupid man, the direktor was about to arrange several sets to be delivered to Bosche as well when Steinhauser spoke again. "You there!" he barked. The group turned, looking for the object of his attention.

A small man, a factory worker, was crossing the courtyard. He wore threadbare clothes, a blue and white arm-band with the Star of David around his sleeve. Practically dragging himself along, it was obvious even from a distance that he was sobbing; tears fell from his unshaven face.

"You!" The man stopped and looked up. "Come!" Steinhauser commanded.

The man fearfully shuffled over and stopped about ten feet away.

"What is your name?" Steinhauser asked.

The man stared blankly, unresponsive.

"Animals," Bosche muttered under his breath as he shook his head. "They are just—"

Steinhauser held up his hand. "Herman, please," he said. "We must show a degree of sensitivity in these situations." Taking a step closer to the man cowering in front of him, he enunciated, "I asked your name."

"Lamus," he answered.

"Lamus, my friend, why are you so upset? See here, you are crying like a child."

As Steinhauser paused, Lamus interrupted, his words bursting forth in agony. "My wife, Rena, and our two-year-old boy, Samuel, were killed in the evacuation of the ghetto last week." Now, weeping uncontrollably and practically screaming, he said, "My only child was swung by his heels into a wall in front of his mother before she died!"

Steinhauser's eyebrows lifted. "Lamus, I am deeply touched. And fortunately for you, I am a man with the power to act upon my compassion." Turning to the adjutant, he said, "Shoot the Jew so that he may be reunited with his family in heaven."

The officers howled with laughter as Bosche clapped Steinhauser on the back. They moved quickly out of the

yard leaving Lamus, the adjutant, and an openmouthed
direktor standing there. The adjutant smiled and unsnapped
his gleaming leather holster. Removing a Luger, he quickly
worked the action, feeding a bullet into the chamber of the
automatic pistol.

"This cannot be done!" the direktor said forcefully. "You
are interfering with all my discipline here!"

The SS officer sneered, then said to Lamus, "Slip your
pants down to your ankles and start walking."

In a daze, Lamus did as he was told.

"The morale of my workers will suffer," the direktor said
desperately. "Production for *der Vaterland* will be affected!"

The officer aimed the Luger.

"A bottle of schnapps if you don't shoot him!" the
direktor hissed.

A pause . . . and then, *"Stimmt!"* the adjutant replied.
"Done!" He lowered the pistol and placed it back in his
holster.

Lamus continued to drag his trousers along behind him,
moving slowly away, waiting for the bullet in his head that
never came. The adjutant of the SS walked toward the factory
offices to collect his schnapps, still talking cheerfully, his arm
around the shoulders of Herr Direktor Oskar Schindler.

POLAND—MARCH 1944

Itzhak Stern bent over the high bookkeeper's table in his
office. Pen in hand, his papers organized neatly around
him, the thin, gray-haired gentleman with the glasses
perched on top of his head gave every evidence of an
employee hard at work. Even his hand was moving the pen

just above the surface of the balance sheets. His eyes, however, were cut to the left, where he could see through the glass door of the larger adjoining office. There behind a large desk sat the direktor, Herr Schindler.

Stern was an accountant by trade, and had directed the auditing division of a large import-export firm since 1924. After the occupation of Poland in September of 1939, the head of each Jewish business was removed and supplanted by a *Treuhander,* or German trustee. Stern's new boss had been a man named Sepp Aue, who eventually introduced him to Oskar Schindler.

Itzhak did not trust Herr Schindler, not at first; after all the man wore a swastika! Before the outbreak of the war, Poland had been relatively safe for Jews. When Germany invaded, however, an entire population of people was herded into one barbed-wire ghetto. Jewish real-estate holdings were stolen and businesses razed or "sold" to German businessmen. These businessmen would then profit greatly from goods produced by Jewish slave labor. One of these "investors" in the economic future of Poland was the fast-talking, hard-drinking, shameless womanizer, Oskar Schindler.

It was an advantage, Stern knew, to be able to leave the confines of the ghetto and to work all day in the factory. When the deportations from Krakow began, Herr Schindler had instructed Stern to falsify records. Stern was astounded at the sheer audacity of the maneuver . . . and the danger to Schindler himself. Old people were notarized as twenty years younger, babies were listed as adults, and doctors and teachers were indexed as metalworkers and mechanics. Everyone filled a role—on paper—as a craftsman essential to the war effort.

When the final liquidation of the ghetto took place on

March 13, 1943, the factory was shut down. Itzhak, along with the other 370 necessary workers at the enamel plant had been moved to Plaszow, a labor camp outside the city. In Plaszow, hundreds had died or had been sent by rail to Auschwitz—only sixty kilometers away. Two months after the move, Stern fell gravely ill. Receiving word of his former accountant's condition, Schindler had visited. He bribed the guards, showered bottles of illegal booze on the officers, and managed to smuggle in the medicine Stern needed to survive. But what he saw in Plaszow unnerved him.

It was at that point, Itzhak felt, that Herr Schindler had crossed some invisible line. He began to put all his thoughts and efforts into a new enterprise.

Schindler knew that other camps, such as Belzec, Sobibor, and Treblinka, were already closed due to the advance of the Russian front. Their inhabitants had been liquidated to the last Jew—without exception. The same would happen soon to Plaszow.

One evening, Schindler convinced one of his drinking associates—a gruppenführer also named Schindler, but no relation—that Plaszow would be an utterly perfect location to produce weapons for the war effort. "After all," the direktor had argued, "I have Jews here who are already trained in assembly and fabrication." He then placed several hundred thousand German marks in the proper hands, and Plaszow was officially designated and converted into a "war-essential" concentration camp. The factory was housed in a building in the town of Zablocie, several kilometers from Plaszow.

A sadist of the first order, Hauptsturmführer Amon Goethe was the commandant in charge of Plaszow. Every morning for several weeks, Itzhak had watched as the commandant eased onto the bedroom balcony of his villa. Usually shirtless and wearing pajama pants with a cigarette in his mouth, Goethe used a high-powered rifle and scope to shoot children as they played. If another child stopped to look or a parent cried out, he shot that person too. When a worker was deemed to be walking too slowly—or walking too quickly—he targeted him or her as an example to the other workers.

Stern had watched with trepidation and amazement as Herr Schindler created a "friend" in Hauptsturmführer Goethe. The direktor plied him regularly with liquor, women, and cash, finally manipulating Goethe himself into introducing a brilliant idea. Why not house the Schindler Jews at the factory in Zablocie to save time in transportation? That, he reasoned, would increase production. It was a brilliant plan, Schindler agreed.

So now, Itzhak thought, *we number over nine hundred. We sleep in the factory or the barracks next to the building. The guards are bribed, and for the moment, no one is beaten or killed . . .* He placed his pen on the table and feigned a stretch, all the while staring and wondering about Oskar Schindler. *Why is he taking this risk? He has created an oasis in hell.*

At that moment, Schindler looked through the glass door and caught his accountant's gaze. With a hand, he motioned Stern into his office. Entering, Itzhak pushed through the ever-present cloud of cigarette smoke to stand in front of the direktor's messy desk. Scattered papers, an empty vase, and two ashtrays covered the desk's large surface, but Itzhak's eyes were on the odd paperweight Schindler plucked from the clutter.

"And how is your morning progressing, Itzhak?" Schindler leaned back in his chair, momentarily placed the

paperweight on his knee, and lit a cigarette. His suit jacket
was hanging on a coat tree in the corner.

"Everything is in order, if that is your concern, Herr
Direktor."

Schindler took a deep draw on the cigarette and exhaled
loudly. "I suppose that is my concern." Absently, he picked
up a paperweight in front of him, tested its heaviness in his
hand, and said, "Call me Oskar. And sit, please."

"I will sit," Stern said, "but I will not do such a foolish
thing as to call you by your given name."

Nodding, Schindler continued to gaze out the window.
"I need a missive constructed." He glanced at Stern and
gestured with his cigarette. "Have it ready to sign today or
at least by this evening. I will be with Goethe, Scherner, the
gruppenführer will be there . . . as well as the Gestapo roy-
alty," he said sarcastically. "Address it to the Gestapo in the
form of a request. It should read . . . ahhh . . . 'In the interest of continued war production, please send all intercepted
Jewish fugitives to me . . . severely understaffed' . . . something about the desperate need for labor and so on."

Stern adjusted his glasses and wrote as Schindler spoke.
Amazing, he thought. *He is doing it again.* The accountant
had many times heard his direktor sniping at the SS or
Gestapo. "Stop killing my good workers," he'd say. "We've
got a war to win. These things can always be settled later!"
Stern had met dozens of Jews whom Schindler saved in
this way.

Schindler put his feet up on his desk and was alternat-
ing between holding the paperweight and placing it on his
stomach, just above his belt line. He put it on his desk
again, leaned back—and almost immediately leaned forward to pick it up again.

Distracted, Stern peered over his glasses and said, "What is that?"

"What?" Schindler responded.

"Forgive my curiosity," Stern said hesitantly, "but I have wondered about it for some time now. What is the thing in your hand? You pick it up. You put it down and pick it up again. You carry it into my office and leave it on my table. Then you come back to get it as soon as you are out my door."

Schindler shrugged and tossed the object to his employee. "A piece of metal," he said. "I don't know. You're the metalworker, Itzhak. You tell me."

Stern caught it deftly. "I am an accountant."

"No, I have seen your papers. They are in my top drawer right there." Schindler pointed to a filing cabinet and grinned. "You are without a doubt one of the Reich's finest metalworkers."

Both men chuckled.

Stern turned the object over in his hand. It was not very heavy, but definitely a dark metal of some sort. It was rectangular in shape and appeared to have been broken or crushed, though plainly visible on its surface were peculiar indentions on both sides—a design? writing?—that seemed almost familiar. "Where did you get this?"

"It was left on the desk when I bought the enamelware factory in Krakow. Just sitting there on a single piece of notepaper on which someone had written, 'Do something!' An anchor for papers in a breezy office. And, I suppose, it feels good in my hand. So I took it when we left."

Stern cocked his head, a bemused expression on his face. "You didn't bring the big picture on the wall of your wife when you left." He held the item toward Schindler. "But you brought this?"

Schindler stood suddenly, a scowl on his face. He took the object from Stern's hand and walked to the window. "Why are we talking about this? Are there not more serious issues with which we need to deal?" He drew ferociously on the last of the cigarette, then tossed it out the open window.

Stern folded his hands in his lap and was quiet. Finally, he said, "I apologize. It was not my intent to upset you."

"I'm not upset." He put the object on his desk and lit another cigarette. Falling heavily back into his chair, he eyed the paperweight, then glancing sheepishly at the accountant, picked it up again. He frowned. "To be honest, it does make me feel"—Schindler motioned with his hand—"ahh . . . conflicted . . . strange? . . . muddled somehow."

Itzhak furrowed his brow, concerned. "An item? Herr Schindler, you are now simply, and quite honestly, under the same duress as your children." Narrowing his eyes and leaning forward, he said slyly, "You do know that is what they call themselves. *Schindlerjuden.* All your workers refer to each other as 'Schindler's children.'"

"Yes, I have heard."

"They depend on you, you know? And they notice the extra food. And they notice the medicine. We see the villa you have been given, yet you spend every night here. Every single night!"

Schindler heaved a sigh. "Itzhak, if the Gestapo were to come while I was gone—"

Stern interrupted, "I know why you stay here, and so do they. You know what is happening all around us. You know that Mengele is experimenting on children in Block Ten at

Auschwitz. You see the ashes that fall into the courtyard from the ovens, and yet you continue to create directives such as this!" He held up the notes he had taken earlier.

"I am more curious about you, Herr Schindler, than I am about any... metal thing." He gestured toward the object in the direktor's hand. "This is not Western Europe. There, I understand, that by aiding a Jew, one would only join the Jew in imprisonment. Here, these madmen have no inhibitions! They have made it very clear. If you are caught, you will be hung in the town square or put against a wall and shot."

"I am aware of these realities," Schindler said softly.

"Then why?" Stern asked. "Why do you want to risk your life every moment as you do?"

Schindler looked directly at his questioner. "I don't want to."

Stern was puzzled. "Pardon me?"

"I don't want to risk my life. I am not a good man. I have no special affinity for the Jews, Itzhak. I don't even know why I am doing this. I only know that I must. If not me, then who? If not now, when?

"Itzhak, I am a lapsed Catholic. I am not a religious man. Surely you know that, but I do remember my mother quoting a scholar. The words were something like, 'If God had wanted you otherwise, He would have created you otherwise.' But I feel as though I was created one way, and now, somehow, I am not that same person." Schindler paused. He stared at the burning end of his cigarette as he continued.

"I try to tell myself that what I am doing is perfectly logical. After all, if you see a dog about to be crushed under a car, wouldn't you help? And yet, I know that this course is fraught with peril and certainly has no support among my peers." Schindler glanced up at Itzhak and smirked at his little joke. "But at some point, a man must stand and act. Not hesitate. Not consider the danger.

"I bought an enamelware factory in order to get rich on the backs of a cheap Jew labor force. And I did it! I had four million marks in suitcases when we left Krakow. But something happened to me. In any case, I decided to act. So I have two million now."

Schindler sighed as he lit a new cigarette from the glowing end of the other. Then he added offhandedly, "And even that might not be enough."

"Enough for what?"

"Enough to get everyone out of here. The eastern retreat is on in full. Soon, I am sure, we will receive orders to shut down. Everyone will be sent to Auschwitz."

LATER THAT WEEK, SCHINDLER DID RECEIVE WORD that Plaszow and all its subcamps were to be voided. The direktor and his accountant knew exactly what this meant. Emptying the camp into another meant a reduction in overall numbers. It meant death.

Standing in the office entryway late one night, Schindler said to Itzhak, "They are playing their final card. It is time for me to play mine. We will create a force of munitions specialists—on paper of course—workers who can build rockets and bombs. Then I will bribe, plead, lie, reason, and somehow, get authorization for a location. Perhaps into Czechoslovakia . . ."

"Herr Schindler"—Stern shook his head—"this is impossible!"

"Never let me hear you say that word again," Schindler snapped. "When a man puts a limit on possibility, he shrinks his future into a manageable morsel of nothing. At this point, Itzhak, your very life depends upon the accomplishment of what you are considering impossible. You are giving aid and comfort to the enemy in your head. Stop it."

The following morning, Stern had three women and six men standing in Schindler's office. "What is this?" the direktor asked.

"Will money help our cause?" Stern answered with a question of his own.

"Without a doubt," Schindler answered. Smiling gently, not wanting to offend, he asked, "And you *have* money?"

"Of a sort," Stern replied. Motioning to the youngest of the women, he said, "Show him, Elayna."

A painfully thin blond girl, no more than seventeen, leaned her head to the side and, to Schindler's astonishment, removed her glass eye. Hidden in the socket were five diamonds, a ruby, and two emeralds. She offered them to Schindler. "They were my mother's," she said simply. "She was sent to Treblinka."

Schindler thanked her and turned to the others who were also placing jewels on his desk. Confused, he asked, "Where have you kept them?" The women looked down at the floor. The men seemed ashamed or angry. "I'm sorry, I don't understand. Is there a hiding place that you've found? Perhaps—"

"They eat them, Herr Direktor," Stern stated plainly. "They have eaten them over and over again."

Embarrassed, but proud, the nine Jewish workers accepted Schindler's words of gratefulness and began to leave the office. Before they could go, however, Elayna moved slowly toward the direktor's desk. She was peering around Schindler and he instinctively slid out of her way. "May I?" she asked, cautiously indicating the metal item.

"Certainly," he answered, a hint of bewilderment on his face. Everyone in the room had stopped.

The girl knelt beside the desk and gently picked up the object. She seemed to contemplate the item for a long moment. Then her countenance changed and she lifted her head, directing a strange, questioning expression to Schindler.

"It's a paperweight," he said, somewhat defensively, and looked at Stern, confused. "It's just a paperweight."

Elayna smiled gently and replaced the object on the desk. "Bless you," she said. "Thank you and bless you."

OSKAR SCHINDLER SPENT EVERY LAST MARK. HE traded his wife's jewelry, his personal effects—literally everything he had left of value to ensure the final authorization he received in October of 1944. He had secured papers allowing him to move 700 men and 300 women to a factory in Brnenec, Czechoslovakia.

The direktor used smiles and threats, chutzpah and promises along the way and added several additional groups, bringing the total of *Schindlerjuden* to 1,098. The other 25,000 men, women, and children from Plaszow were sent to Auschwitz to experience the fate of the several million who had gone before them.

The factory in Brnenec, just as Herr Schindler had envisioned, produced bombs and rocket loads for the Wehrmacht until they were liberated by the end of the war seven months later. However, during that time, not one single munition passed the quality tests established by the German military.

There was a moment, however, during the chaos of departure from Plaszow that Itzhak Stern remembered for the rest of his life. At the rail yard, Itzhak was packed into a cattle container with the others who had been saved. This train, thankfully, was headed away from Auschwitz and toward the factory in Czechoslovakia. He was so tightly squeezed into the dirty, damp car that he could barely move and hardly breathe, when suddenly, he heard his friend calling frantically. "Itzhak! Itzhak Stern!"

"Here, Herr Schindler! I am here!" Itzhak managed to move his face into a small hole in order to be seen.

The direktor smiled with clenched teeth. He was in a panic. "Itzhak," he said forcefully. "I left the paperweight in my office. I think I want to go back." He glanced around quickly. "I think I want to." He fumbled for a cigarette. "But I can't go back. If I leave everyone now . . ."

As Schindler urgently babbled, Stern maneuvered his body in the crowded rail car. For a moment, his face disappeared.

"Itzhak!" Schindler beat his fist on the car. "Are you there?"

Slowly a hand came out of the hole. It was the hand of Itzhak Stern and in it was the paperweight. As the train began to move, Schindler took it and trotted alongside the train as his friend's smiling face reappeared.

"I went through the office a last time," Itzhak yelled over the noise of the train. "I got it for you!"

"Thank you!" Schindler said as he ran faster to keep up.

"Why do you need it?" Itzhak managed to yell as the train gathered momentum and pulled away.

Oskar stopped. Before he moved to the automobile that was to be his transportation, he looked at the object in his hand and lifted his eyebrows. Placing it in the left jacket pocket of his gray, double-breasted suit, he shook his head and said, "I don't know. I really don't know."

⫷ THREE

THE DENVER MUSEUM OF NATURE AND SCIENCE is one of the finest examples of functional academia in the world. Its massive, four-story presence at 2001 Colorado Boulevard is a monument to the centuries of knowledge gathered and filed in the categories of anthropology, zoology, and earth sciences. The museum is also a repository for important historical documents and photographs. These particular items are guarded by an extremely well organized staff known to the outside world as the Library and Archives group.

Dylan Langford was keenly aware of the power wielded by these people. He had once even baked cookies for them. "Don't wait until you need Library and Archives to be nice to them," he had been told early in his career. "It'll be too late." He knew from experience that if there was even a tiny harbored grudge, they could turn into the dumbest people on the planet, unable to find anything or answer any question.

Kendra Harper's youngest brother, Dylan, had only been at the museum for several months. He was twenty-nine years old and on the fast track with his career. Well over six feet tall and rail thin, his prematurely graying hair and receding hairline gave the appearance of an older man. Dylan cultivated that perception, knowing that the world of anthropology and archaeology was rife with competition in its ranks, and young people in his field were often overlooked for advancement.

Dylan was now a full-fledged curator of anthropology. Though not the department head, he was free to pursue his own course of study. He was certainly qualified. After receiving his BA from the University of Nebraska, he had earned an MA and finally, his PhD in anthropology from Johns Hopkins.

His office was not big, but it was nicer than most of the interior "cubbyholes" on the third floor. It was a "cubbyhole" with a nameplate on the door, which, at the moment, was open. The office boasted a wall-sized world map and a huge desk circa 1970-something-or-other. Behind the desk a computer station jutted out from a wall of bookshelves that were filled with research manuals and college textbooks that he hadn't been able to sell and was too cheap to throw away. His rolling chair was the only one in his office—not counting the folding chair stored behind the door—and often, he gleefully spun like a kid from his desk to the computer station.

Dylan glanced at his watch and pushed back from his computer as he turned an entire circle in the short distance back to his desk. *Almost two o'clock,* he thought. He drummed his hands on his desktop. Dylan hated it when people were late. Not that Dorry was . . . yet.

His sister had called and cleared the way for her next-door neighbor, Dorry Chandler, to make contact. "She's nice and fun and all that, Dylan," Kendra had said, "and I love her dearly. But just so you know, she is a reporter, and she has one of those kind of . . . um . . . you know, rabid personalities." He wasn't exactly sure what his sister had meant by "rabid" personality, but felt that he might have one too.

"Hello?" Dorry stuck her head in and smiled. "Dylan?" She wore jeans and a pink Polo shirt that made her red hair look as if it were on fire.

"Dorry. Hi," he said as he rose from his chair and moved around the desk, sneaking a look at his watch. "You're on time."

"You said 2:00. It's 2:00. *I* am on time! Believe me, if it had been 2:01, I'd have called."

Dylan laughed. "Last of a breed."

"No," Dorry smirked, "evidently, there's still you."

Dylan laughed again. He liked her. "Yep, there's still me. Hey, I enjoyed meeting you and your husband the other night. Mark, right?"

"Yeah, good memory. You know, Mark has the 'on time thing' too. He's a detective with DPD so that goes with the territory." Dylan nodded. "I really appreciate you taking the time to see me, Dylan. It's more of a curiosity deal than anything, I suppose, but you're the only person I know who works in a museum, so . . ."

Dylan was used to that particular line of thought. *You work in a museum! You must know everything.* It was funny to him. People treated the janitor the same way. After all, he worked in a museum too. *Excuse me, sir, I know you're waxing the floors right now, but during what paleontological period did DNA manifest itself to bring about a broadening of the species?*

It was incredible. Dylan wondered if they treated other professions the same way.

"Well," he said, "let's see what you have."

As Dorry dug through her purse, Dylan retrieved the chair from behind the door and unfolded it. "Have a seat. Sorry, it's kind of cramped in here."

"Bigger than my office," Dorry remarked as she produced the object from her purse.

Dylan took the object, glanced up at Dorry briefly, and moved around behind his desk. Seemingly transfixed by what he was seeing, he slowly lowered himself into his chair and turned on a small lamp attached to some sort of magnification device. Frowning, he said, "You got this where?"

"My son found it. Basically in our backyard."

Dylan looked up, a bemused expression on his face. "Oh, come on. Seriously?"

"Yeah. Why?"

"I don't know," he said casually. "I suppose it's not just every day one comes across a Mesopotamian relic beside someone's patio in Denver."

"What?!"

Dylan chuckled. "I don't mean to be melodramatic. Frankly, the piece is not *totally* unusual . . . I don't think. I just happen to recognize it because there are fifty jillion pieces just like it in museums all over the world . . . The question mark is with your kid finding it where he did." Dylan paused. "And there's this script, too, of course . . ."

"So that *is* some kind of writing?"

"Uh-huh." Dylan ran his fingernail into the grooves. "I don't recognize it, but I'll pass this on and find out what's what. We should know more in a week or two."

"Two?" Dorry's eyes were wide-open. "I just thought

we might be able . . . I mean that you could . . . two weeks?"

Dylan smiled, stood up, and came around to Dorry's side of the desk. "Look"—he shrugged—"this kind of thing is not in my area of expertise. I've got some buddies though. We'll figure it out."

Dorry stood and nodded. "Okay, thanks. That makes sense. I'm just sort of a 'right now' person, you know. And I thought, *hey, he works in a museum . . ."*

Dylan smiled.

After Dorry left, Dylan shut the door and went back to his desk. Sitting down, he began slowly swinging the chair back and forth with his foot. Dylan stared blankly at the map on the wall, not really taking it in, but lost in thought—only occasionally glancing at the object still in his hands. *So a kid finds this in his backyard,* Dylan thought. *Kinda weird, kinda not.*

No one could ever know with certainty how any particular relic came to lie in a particular place—it was one of the enduring mysteries of his profession and purely guesswork. Origins, however, were easier to pinpoint. For instance, no one knew how the obsidian pottery with elaborate faces formed into the edges ended up in one hundred feet of water off the Pacific coast. Archaeologists were, however, able to determine that they were more than three thousand years old and came from Southeast Asia.

Moving the chair closer to his desk, Dylan shook his head sharply to clear the cobwebs and placed the object in his hand under the magnifying light. Mentally, he plodded through what he knew. *Almost certainly leaded bronze. A cast piece, no carving except the script. Script is clearly etched. No staining or corrosion evident. Is that unusual? I don't know.*

For a full minute or more Dylan sat completely still, then he opened the drawer by his right knee. Carefully, he removed a small electronic scale and placed it next to the light on his desk. Plugging it into an adapter on the base of the lamp, he turned the scale on and placed the object onto its measuring pan. Dylan pressed the buttons "Clear" and "Zero," then watched as the digital numbers 139.22 appeared in green. *Hmmm. Okay. A little more than 139 grams . . . almost five ounces.* He pulled a small tape measure from the drawer in front of him—*4¾ inches long and . . . 1⅞ inches at its widest point.*

Dylan leaned back in his chair, faced the map, and began moving back and forth again. He reviewed what he knew, which was not much. *I am an anthropologist, not an archaeologist.* Dylan smiled. Most people, he knew, did not know the difference. He had to explain it to his own mother every time he was home for a holiday. Archaeologists studied ancient civilizations, whereas he, an anthropologist, was concerned with the human beings themselves—their environment, social interaction, and culture.

Dylan's particular area of proficiency was directed toward the Plains Indians of the early 1800s. *Show me an arrowhead, I'll tell you what they ate for dinner.* He turned to look at the object on the scale. *But I don't know jack about this!* Suddenly he stood up, grabbed the object, and slipping it into his pants pocket, headed to the door. *I may not know anything,* he smiled to himself, *but I know some archys who do!*

TWO WEEKS LATER, DORRY SAT IN TRAFFIC AS SHE left downtown Denver. She kept a wary eye on the sports car trying to ease in front of her as she fished the chirping cell phone from her purse. Seeing "HOME" on the display, she punched "Send" and answered. "Is this my big boy or my little boy?"

On the other end of the line, Mark chuckled. "This is your big boy. Why do you ask?"

"Because if it was my little boy," Dorry said wryly, "I didn't want him to hear his mother screaming like a lunatic."

"Traffic?"

"Yep. I just might kill somebody in a couple of minutes."

"Don't tell me that. I'm a cop."

Dorry laughed. "If I had known cops worked shifts and got off at three in the afternoon, I'd never have gone to journalism school. I'd have been running the obstacle course at the academy with you."

"Yeah, well, you didn't think so much of the job when I was eleven-to-seven," Mark replied. Changing the subject, he said, "Hey, what I called about . . . Dylan touched base earlier—Kendra's brother? The guy from the museum?"

"Really?" Dorry said, her mood changing instantly despite the traffic. "What did he say?"

"Nothing really," Mark said. "He told me he was headed out our way tonight—I guess to see his sister—anyway, he said he had some info on the object and asked if it was okay to drop by. I told him just to plan on eating dinner with us." There was silence on the phone. "Dorry?"

"Yes?" Her mood had changed again. "Mark, I won't be home till after seven o'clock! I have an article to write tonight . . . Dinner? What time is he coming?"

"Well, I told him . . . seven . . . -ish. Tell you what: Michael and I will cook. You won't have to do a thing."

"Uh-huh," Dorry said through clenched teeth. "696-8777."

"What?" Mark asked.

"I said, 696-8777. It's the number for Domino's. Just get whatever."

"Okay."

"Mark?"

"Yes?

"No anchovies."

AFTER DINNER THAT EVENING, MARK PRESIDED OVER Michael's bath and got him into bed while Dorry made coffee and engaged in small talk with Dylan. When at last they were all in the living room, Mark asked, "Well, is this gonna be good or did we waste your time?"

"Good, I think," Dylan grinned. "Intriguing anyway. Are you ready?" Mark and Dorry nodded. "All right, here goes."

Dylan pulled the object out of a satchel he'd brought in and left on the couch earlier.

"Well . . . ," Dylan began, "I gave it to an archy down the hall from me . . . an archaeologist," he added, noting the quizzical expressions on the Chandlers' faces. "Her name is Abby. She's nice. Cute, which is a plus. And she said 'yes' when I asked her out, which is another plus." Dylan looked up and smiled before continuing. "She's new to Denver and the museum, like me, and being young, is anxious to prove her PhD is not a fluke."

"So what did she say?" Dorry pushed.

"Hang on, I'm getting there," Dylan answered. He pulled a palm-sized personal computer from his satchel, clicked a few buttons with a plastic pencil, and said, "Leaded bronze."

Dylan looked up. "You know, I thought it was leaded bronze, but this is really old stuff. I mean really old. Not Bronze Age exactly, but almost."

Mark leaned forward. "Which means what? How old?"

"Less than twenty-four hundred years old, but almost certainly older than eighteen hundred. Old."

"You're kidding," Dorry said.

"Nope. Could be only sixteen . . . seventeen hundred years, but Abby doubts it. She said the quality of the casting is not that great, which would skew it older. It's soft, she says, though it doesn't feel soft to me." All three of them looked at the object on the coffee table. "*Soft* is a relative term with metals, I suppose."

Dylan continued. "Bronze is an alloy—an amalgamation of metals—originally created by adding tin to copper. Copper was too brittle to use for anything other than ornamentation."

Dylan looked at his computer again. "Lead was deliberately added to the mix during this period to lower the melting temperature and facilitate pouring and molding. When this was made"—Dylan bent forward and picked up the object from the table—"leaded bronze was mostly for statues, pots, some weapons. And—I thought this was interesting—leaded bronze coins were used by the Roman Empire during the same time period as the casting of this particular piece."

"Wow!" Dorry exclaimed. "Did she know where it came from?"

Dylan scrunched up his face, closing one eye. "Hard to tell from the composition. Listen to the list of places that made this kind of thing during that time period." He punched a button on the computer with his thumb. "Babylonia, Egypt, Greece, Mesopotamia, China, Persia, and most of Europe." Dylan smiled. "Tough to narrow anything down with that list . . . but you haven't asked about the script!"

Mark and Dorry unconsciously moved closer to Dylan. "Was she able to actually translate that?" Mark asked.

"Wait a minute," Dylan chuckled. "The words are Aramaic." Noting the frowns on the faces of his friends, Dylan explained. "Aramaic is actually a grouping or combination of languages known almost from the beginning of recorded history. It includes Arabic, Hebrew, and Ethiopic, as well as Akkadian from Babylonia and Syria. Our first glimpse of this written style appeared around 900 BC.

"Portions of the Bible and all of the Dead Sea Scrolls were written in Aramaic, and we have surviving doctrinal works from Sumaria in this same script. Believe it or not, Aramaic is still a spoken language in parts of Syria, Iraq, Turkey, Iran, and Lebanon." Dylan smiled broadly and held up the object. "So you see. It was not hard to translate."

"So you *were* able to translate it!" Mark said.

"Well, Abby was able to," Dylan responded. "You wanna know what it says?"

"Yes!" Mark and Dorry answered in unison.

"Okay. It doesn't make much sense, but it's kinda interesting. In any case, it translates as 'By your hand, the people shall live.' "

For a moment, all three were silent. Dylan put the object back on the coffee table. Mark picked it up. "Huh. By your hand, the people shall live."

Dorry held out her hand and waggled her fingers at Mark. "Let me see it." Mark gave it to her. "What's that mean?" she asked Dylan.

He shrugged. "Don't know. And we probably never will. It is an enigma that belongs in the same category as how it ended up in your backyard."

As they talked, Dylan told stories of the ancient finds

that had been made over the years on the North American continent. Coins from the Roman Empire had shown up in Missouri, Oklahoma, and Alabama, and an Egyptian-minted Gallenius coin was found by geology students in a streambed near Black Mountain, North Carolina. A Chinese ship found in thirty feet of clay near Sacramento was carbon-dated over one thousand years old. A cave discovered in southern Illinois in 1982 yielded stones engraved with ancient Semitic script and portraits of Egyptians, Romans, and Hebrews. "And no one has any idea how any of this stuff got here," Dylan said.

It was almost ten o'clock when Dorry grudgingly announced the end of their evening. Explaining her work situation and the article to be written by morning, she and Mark walked Dylan to the door. "Thanks so much, Dylan. We really appreciate your time on this," she said. "And please thank Abby too."

"No problem," he answered, "and I will thank Abby. By the way, I forgot to mention this. The thing is hollow."

"What?" Mark asked.

"Yeah, no big deal really. But she ran a scope on it—radio waves, direct light-beam attachments—and it's hollow! Anyway, thanks for the pizza, and keep in touch, okay?" They assured him that they would.

Within the hour, Dorry was writing, Mark was asleep, and the object of the evening's discussion lay on the coffee table—a unique souvenir, a conversation piece . . . a relic from the ditch.

❧ FOUR

MARK, DORRY, AND MICHAEL HAD EATEN BRUNCH earlier than usual. Scrambled eggs, bacon *and* sausage, real waffles (not the kind from the freezer) with blueberries, orange juice, and coffee. It was the same menu Mark prepared every Saturday. The only wild card was the fruit that went into the waffles. Sometimes strawberries or bananas, but blueberries were Michael's favorite, so most times they ate blueberries.

Mark sat at the breakfast table scanning the newspaper while Dorry cleaned the kitchen and drank her fourth cup of coffee. This, too, was a Saturday tradition. Mark cooked the food; Dorry cleaned up the mess. Michael was in the recliner watching cartoons, but Mark always stayed in the kitchen and read to his wife. "Do you have anything in here today?"

"Uh-huh," Dorry said as she rinsed a plate and placed it in the dishwasher. "It should be in the first section."

"And it is about . . . ?" Mark turned the pages quickly, searching for his wife's byline.

City council voting on sign restrictions for small businesses and the redistricting of school board members. I'm sure you'll want to cut it out and frame it."

"Here it is." Mark spread out the paper on the table. "Page fourteen—Dorry Chandler. Do I have to read it?"

"No, but if you'll let *me* read it, I'll be able to go back to sleep."

"Boring, huh?"

"Unbelievably."

"It sounds boring."

"You're very perceptive," Dorry said as she closed the dishwasher and pressed the START button. She poured another cup of coffee and sat down across from Mark. "What else is in there? Read to me."

"Okay . . .," Mark said. "Let's see . . . what should we read? Sports? Hard news? Sports? International news? Lifestyles? Or . . . sports?"

"Anything but sports," Dorry said, taking a sip of her coffee.

"The Broncos' offensive coordinator is upset about the turf conditions for tomorrow's game."

"Tragic. Next."

"The Rockies and the Braves are talking about an off-season trade."

"A trade?! I know *my* life will change. Excuse me," Dorry said banging her spoon on the side of her coffee cup. "Excuse me, Marky, but was it someone else to whom I made the request 'anything but sports'?"

Mark tried to suppress a smile. "What? Oh! I'm sorry, dear. You're right. Let me find some dull, humdrum, mind-numbing articles we can enjoy together!" He grabbed another section with a flourish.

"Sheesh! Here's a picture of a woman who is 104 years old."

"No way!"

"Mm-hmm. Mrs. Bonnie Mae Bounds of Fordyce, Arkansas. The cutline on the picture says she's 104. And she doesn't look a day over a hundred."

"Funny. You want some coffee?"

"Sure."

Dorry stood and stretched. Before pouring the coffee, she glanced at the picture of the old woman. There was no accompanying article. It was wire service filler, sent to newspapers as human interest, for use on slow news days. The photograph was large—almost one-eighth of a page. Bonnie Mae Bounds, an African-American woman with snow-white hair, was seated in a wooden, high-backed rocking chair with a shawl draped across her lap. The photo had been taken indoors, presumably in her home. There was, Dorry saw, a painting of a house on the wall over her right shoulder and a bookshelf directly behind her. Though the picture was in black and white, Dorry imagined that the long dress she wore was a dark green or blue.

"Gee. A hundred and four." Dorry stepped over to the counter to get the coffeepot.

Mark turned the page. Then another couple of pages. "Swim lessons are opening for five-year-olds at the Y. We want to do that, don't we?" Mark looked up. "Dorry?"

Dorry was standing at the counter beside the refrigerator. She had her back to Mark, the coffeepot in her hand, and was not moving a muscle. When Mark said her name, she turned around with a quizzical expression on her face. "Turn back to that picture," she said.

"What?"

Dorry turned again, placing the coffeepot in its holder.

"The photo of the old lady, turn back to it." She walked back to him.

"Why do you—," he began as he reached to thumb through the paper.

"Mark!" she interrupted and made a "hurry up!" motion with her hand.

"Okay!" he replied. "Okay. Here." He smoothed the newspaper and tilted it toward her.

Dorry got on her knees beside her husband and picked up the page in order to angle it into the light. Her eyebrows raised as her mouth dropped open. "Did you see this?" she asked simply and put the paper back on the table. She sat down on the floor and looked at Mark. "Did you?"

Totally confused by his wife's reaction, Mark frowned. "What? Did I see what?"

Dorry rose to her feet without a word. She moved the newspaper back to face Mark and placed her finger on the photo. Mark leaned over and followed the direction of Dorry's point. For a long moment, he stared. Then, he straightened and said, "You have got to be kidding."

For several seconds they gaped at each other. Mark spoke first. "Let me see that again." He grabbed the newspaper and, walking to the window, folded it thickly so that virtually the only thing showing was the photograph. He held it into the light. The bookshelf behind the old woman was filled with knickknacks and small framed photographs in addition to the books. But unmistakably, there on the shelf just beside Mrs. Bonnie Mae Bounds' left elbow was an object exactly like the one Michael had found several months earlier in their backyard.

Mark turned the photograph this way and that as if he might get a closer view as Dorry hurried to the living room and snatched *their* relic from the coffee table. Returning to the kitchen, she stood close to Mark and held the object up next to the picture. "What do you think?" she asked.

"Well"—Mark spoke cautiously—"it sure looks like the one we have. But Dylan did say that pieces like this were not uncommon."

"Yeah, but this is identical," Dorry argued. "Look—you can even see the writing."

After a moment Mark said, "So, what do we do now? Do you want to find out about it?"

"Yes, I want to find out about it! Aren't *you* curious? I mean, why are there two of these things? And why does a 104-year-old woman have one? Let me see the pic again." She reached for the paper. "I didn't notice . . . is it AP?" She looked. "It is AP. Okay, the *Post* will have a record of the date and time it came over the wire. I can track the photographer that way. Maybe we can get an address or phone number for her."

"She won't be hard to find," Mark said. "How many 104-year-old people could there be in Fordyce, Arkansas?"

ON THE FOLLOWING TUESDAY, FROM HER DESK IN the newsroom at the *Post,* Dorry talked by phone with Braxton Pringle, a young-sounding employee of the *Fordyce News-Advocate.* Braxton was the photographer/reporter responsible for the picture that Mark and Dorry had seen.

After discovering Dorry was a journalist, and with the *Denver Post,* Braxton enthusiastically gave Dorry the woman's address—1022 Jug Creek Road—and then proceeded to pepper her with questions about journalism. It was, he told her, his passion.

After patiently answering questions for several minutes, Dorry guided the conversation back to Bonnie Mae Bounds. "I'm interested in something I saw in the picture you took, something on the bookshelf behind her," she explained.

"I remember that bookshelf. Lotta junk there," Braxton said. "Anyway, you know how to get in touch if you think of a way I can help. Keep our number, okay?"

"I will, Braxton. And you hang in there! You're going to make a great reporter."

That evening at dinner Mark and Dorry could talk about nothing else but Bonnie Mae Bounds, the object on her bookshelf, and what it could possibly be—considering the fact that they had a duplicate in their living room. So it was a natural unfolding of events that occurred when Mark mentioned he had to fly to Memphis the following week. Four times in the last two months, he'd had to leave home in order to work with police departments in other cities regarding situations of mutual concern. Chicago, Salt Lake, Memphis, and Memphis again. Mark had developed a degree of specialization in cases involving missing persons and was often called for help of one kind or another, particularly those that involved kids. This was one of those cases—two children, a brother and sister from Denver's suburbs, who had been missing for months.

Within an hour of the realization that Mark was indeed headed yet again to Memphis, Dorry had checked on the Internet to find that Fordyce was less than a four-hour drive from there. With that information and a go-ahead from Mark, she reserved a rental car from Hertz, used Sky Miles to get a round-trip ticket on the same flight as her husband, and talked to her parents about keeping Michael. She could hardly wait. They were going to Arkansas.

⊰ FIVE

IT WAS A CLASSIC CASE OF "HURRY UP AND WAIT." And waiting was not an easy thing for Dorry Chandler to do.

Eight days after her conversation with Braxton Pringle, their flight had taken off on time at 7:52 Wednesday morning, but that was two days ago. So here it was Friday and she was waiting again. Mark was using the rental car, so she was stuck by herself in a hotel on a service road of I-40 that was located next to . . . nothing.

They would drive on to Fordyce this afternoon and check into a hotel there. Tomorrow—Saturday—was all blocked out to spend whatever time they could with Mrs. Bounds. *Mark should be back anytime,* Dorry thought as she flopped onto the unmade bed and contemplated taking a shower. Instead, she got back up and poured the last of the coffee from the room's pot and started a new one brewing.

When Mark arrived, Dorry was showered, dressed,

53

packed, and ready to roll. "Okay!" she said clapping her hands together and heading for the door. "Let's do it!"

"Hey, Dorry! Give me a second to take a breath! At least say 'hello' or something!"

"You're right," she said, walking over and giving him a hug. "I'm sorry—I've just been bored out of my mind!"

"I'm not sure the boredom caused that," Mark pouted. "Give me just a minute and we'll get out of here. Have you eaten lunch?"

"No," she replied. "I thought we'd grab something on the way. How did it go with your meetings?"

"It didn't," Mark said from the bathroom. "This is my last trip to Memphis—for this case anyway. Trust me, those kids are not here. Not that I have any clue where to go next . . ." He cursed. It was one word, under his breath, but loud enough for Dorry to hear from where she was sitting on the bed.

She studied Mark as he emerged from the bathroom, toweling water from his face. She was well aware that he took every case personally. The ones that ended badly or continued past a certain point with little progress sometimes made him physically ill. Dorry worried about him, especially when he dealt with missing children.

But less than an hour later, Mark was back to his old self. Before the green Ford Taurus hit the on-ramp to the interstate, they had connected with Dorry's mother and Michael. The two had just come back from a movie, and Dorry silently said a "thank-you prayer" that they had been home when she called. Michael jabbered away, telling his dad all about the movie as Dorry watched Mark's anxiety melt away. By the time they hung up, Mark was beaming.

FORDYCE, ARKANSAS

"It's raining," Mark said as he opened the hotel room curtains the next morning. "Do you want me to get my shower first?" Dorry did not move. "Dorry. Wake up. It's seven-thirty. Do you want me to go ahead and take my shower?"

Dorry never understood why Mark didn't just *take a shower!* Why was it, she wondered, that he felt the need to get her permission? Just take it! Do it! Be first, she wanted to scream! *Be my guest!*

"Dorry . . . are you awake?" Mark shook her lightly. "I'll go ahead and take my shower, okay?"

Dorry clenched her teeth and mumbled, "Great."

"What did you say?"

Dorry almost levitated off the bed into Mark's face. "I said 'take a shower.' Take it!" she said and fell back, flinging the covers over her head in one swift move.

"Gee!" Mark said as he hurried away. "What's wrong with you?"

Fifteen minutes later, Mark emerged carefully from the bathroom. He slowly eased his head around the corner to see his wife sitting in the lounge chair beside the bed. She had a cup of coffee in her hand and a smile on her face. "Good morning, dear," she said sweetly.

Mark made a show of glancing around the room. "Is it you?" he asked. "I want to make sure, you know, because a few minutes ago there was a psychopath in the bed."

"That wasn't me, dear," Dorry said. "That was Doraine. See?" She held her cup toward Mark. "It's me, Dorry. You know that mean old Doraine doesn't drink coffee."

This was one of Mark and Dorry's games of apology. No need to hash things out in a long, drawn-out examination

of who said what, who said it first, or why. Harsh words?
Blame it on Doraine—Dorry's evil twin. It was simple, it
was quick, and it worked.

After coffee and muffins in the hotel lobby, they ran
through the parking lot to the Taurus. The temperature was
in the midforties, which added to the miserable conditions
as they scrambled across the uneven asphalt, avoiding huge
puddles of water. Mark clutched a piece of paper in his
fist—directions to Mrs. Bounds' house, given to them over
the phone by Braxton, the boy who worked at the local
newspaper.

Soon Mark and Dorry had the Taurus nosing along Jug
Creek Road. "Didn't Braxton say she lived across from the
church?" Mark asked. "Well, there it is."

He parked the car next to the curb across the street from
the Mount Zion Baptist Church in front of a small, freshly
painted house with dark green shutters that matched the
porch. The numbers above the door, 1022, confirmed the
location. Dorry took a deep breath.

Mark laughed. "Are you nervous?"

"I am!" she replied. "I have interviewed the governor
and wasn't nervous, so I'm not sure why I feel this way
now. But it seems important somehow. Let's go," she said
and got out of the car.

As they walked up the neat brick walkway to the house,
Mark pointed out the fall garden that grew in the side yard.
Despite the cool weather, it was lush with turnips, cauli-
flower, beets, carrots, huge collards—even tomatoes still
hung from their vines. And not a weed to be seen.
Climbing the steps to the porch, they noticed that the
flower beds on either side of the steps were planted in vege-
tables as well.

"The whole neighborhood must eat from this garden," Dorry whispered. Mark nodded in agreement. They stood facing a front door festooned with an autumnal wreath. Bright-yellow ornamental gourds intertwined with red and black Indian corn hung on the clean, white wood surface. There was no doorbell, so Dorry knocked.

Almost immediately, the door slowly swung open to reveal a tiny, old woman with hair like ivory. Her black eyes danced against the contrast of her skin, which was a shade of dark caramel. Dorry was about to introduce herself when the old lady broke into a grin and said, "Oh, girl! I can tell we gon' be friends. You da same size as me!"

Dorry's eyes widened, Mark tried to suppress a sudden snicker, then they all burst into laughter. The woman opened the door wide and said, "Come on in now. We lettin' my heat out."

As they entered, Dorry said, "Mrs. Bounds, I'm Dorry Chan—"

"Hold on, baby," interrupted the old woman. "Firs' of all, I'm Mae Mae. Mrs. Bounds is my mama and she been dead for eighty-seven years. So you and the police call me Mae Mae."

Dorry's eyes were wide again. She stole a look at Mark who appeared on the verge of laughter again after the "police" remark. Mae Mae had pronounced the word "PO-leese."

"Second thing is," she continued, "I already know who you are. You are Dorry, and you"—she smiled at Mark—"you the police! But I'm gon' call you Mark. Now get on in here." And with that, she turned and shuffled into her small living room.

"Sit down right there, baby." Mae Mae directed Dorry

to a couch. "Mark, you go in the kitchen—right throug
door—and get this little girl whatever she wants to drink.
me a cup of coffee. I like it black. Pot's on the stove."

Dorry smiled up at her husband from the couch. "I
have coffee too, Mark," she said and thought his eyebrows
might merge with his hairline—he appeared to be that surprised. But meekly, he mumbled a "yes, ma'am" and went
through the door Mae Mae had indicated.

Dorry watched as the old woman eased herself into the
same rocking chair she had seen in the newspaper. Next to
the rocking chair was the source of brutal heat, an old gas
heater. Oblivious to the temperature inside the house,
which Dorry judged to be almost eighty degrees, a plain
white sweater was draped across her shoulders.

Dorry was surprised—almost to the point of shock—
that a woman as old as Mae Mae didn't appear to be as
decrepit as she'd imagined. Her face was wrinkled, but not
to an extreme, and her posture, though somewhat stooped,
seemed excellent. Even the skin on her hands was devoid
of the age spots afflicting Dorry's own mother, who was
still in her sixties, and Mae Mae's hair, though bone white,
was thick and healthy. It was braided and rolled into a bun
on the back of her head. Dorry had also noted that her
movements were slow, but not those of a person tormented
by arthritis or rheumatism.

Directly behind her was the bookcase, including the
object that had prompted the trip. Dorry had spotted it the
minute she walked into the room. The relic was propped on
a tiny framing easel and—something the newspaper photograph had not revealed—was attached to a stiff leather cord.

"You have a nice place, Mae Mae," Dorry began. "How
long have you lived here?"

"This Christmas, it'll be forty-one years," she answered. "My husband built this old house with his brother. Jus' the two of 'em. It was a pretty place. Jerold passed on not long after that . . . seventy years old . . . still a young man. Lord, I loved that Jerold."

"Do you have children?"

"No, baby. We never did. Mae Mae got no family a'tall. All Jerold's people . . . an' my side too—they gone. But the folks in Fordyce see after Mae Mae. This house paint—my pretty porch—tha's all the sweetness of this town. They's a little white boy even come cut Mae Mae's grass."

Mark entered with a cup of coffee in each hand and presented one to the old lady, then to Dorry, and accepted their thanks.

"Mrs. Bounds," Dorry began.

"Mae Mae," the old woman said.

"Mae Mae . . ." Dorry was suddenly nervous again. "When we saw your picture in the paper, we were curious about that . . . thing." She pointed to the object on the bookshelf.

Mae Mae twisted in her chair and, with a questioning glance, picked up the item her guest had indicated. "This?" she asked, holding it up for them to see.

For the next few minutes, Mae Mae sat quietly as the Chandlers told her the story of the relic their son had found. They showed her pictures of Michael and their home. Finally, Dorry removed their object from her purse. She unwrapped it from a handkerchief and saw Mae Mae's eyebrows raise as Dorry placed it in her hands.

Neither Mark nor Dorry had gotten a close look at the item from Mae Mae's shelf. Mark was hesitant to be too pushy. Years of training and experience as a detective had convinced him that it was a mistake to move too quickly. It often caused a person to close up, even become frightened— though he wasn't sure anyone could frighten *this* woman.

He put his arm around Dorry's shoulder and eased her back as Mae Mae examined the two pieces. *Easy . . . slow down,* he directed his thoughts to his wife. "Mae Mae? Can I get you some more coffee?" Mark said as he purposefully stood. "I know Dorry could use some." He shot Dorry a look that said, *be careful,* and walked to the kitchen after both women gave him their cups.

The silence from the living room was deafening as Mark poured the coffee. Returning with the now filled cups, Mark smiled at Dorry, sitting stiffly on the couch. She was watching the old woman's every move. Mae Mae had a habit of rolling her dentures around in her mouth when she was deep in thought. Mark had noted the tendency earlier, but now, the plates were clicking audibly. Her concentration appeared to be absolute as she turned the pieces first one way, then another. "What do you think, Mae Mae?" Mark said softly as he sat back down.

She jerked her head up as if she had forgotten they were there. "Sho look like another food stone," she said and reached toward Dorry to pass the objects to her. "See what you reckon, baby."

Dorry took the pieces, but before she gave them the barest glimpse, Mark asked the obvious question for both of them. "What did you call it, Mae Mae? A 'food stone'?"

"Tha's right. It look just like my granddaddy's food stone."

Dorry examined the two objects, which, as far as she could tell, were almost identical. The only difference she could discern was a degree of variation on the edges—one side was rounded, curled over as if one had folded a piece of bread—and a slight alteration in the script. And, of course, there was the attached leather cord. Dorry could see that in the corner of the object, a small opening—a natural one, she assumed—had been bored completely through to the other side, creating a tiny tunnel through which the cord ran.

"Did you get this from your grandfather?" Mark continued gently.

"No," Mae Mae said taking a sip of her coffee. "I got it after my Uncle Gee passed on. It was left to him by my granddaddy. He had it 'round his neck when they brought him over from Africa." Dorry started to ask a question, but Mark nudged her, urging silence in hopes that the old woman would continue to talk. She did.

"My daddy was called James. He was from Missouri and died with the smallpox when I was a baby girl. Not a lot of paper on black folk back then, but he was 'posed to been twenty-one or two when he passed. What with Daddy gone, Uncle Gee took that place in my life. He stood up for me when I married Jerold. Uncle Gee was there for me till he passed on hisself in nineteen hundred and forty-three." Mae Mae paused, remembering. She nodded to herself and squinted as if examining the image in her mind's eye. As Mark and Dorry waited, she finished her coffee and then, seemingly struck by a recollection, Mae Mae leaned forward and motioned for the object.

Taking it from Dorry, she draped the cord over her wrist and held it up to the light. "I ain't nevah changed this string," she said. "Tha's the same strip of leather my Uncle Gee wore. Might be the same one my granddaddy wore. Uncle Gee sho kep it roun' his neck like his daddy." Earlier, noticing the hole where the cord passed through the object,

Dorry had recalled Dylan's assertation that the object *he* had inspected was hollow.

"The story I know from my mama is . . . when the slave catchers brought my granddaddy to America, he had it on 'im. And for some reason, they never took it! Took ever' thing else, but left a rock hangin' on the man's neck. Sold 'im in Baton Rouge. Stood 'im on the auction block naked as a jaybird. Took the man's clothes—but didn' touch that rock. Ever."

"Uncle Gee tol' me that his daddy—my granddaddy— had it on till the day he got killed. Killed in a loggin' accident in Missouri. 'Course, some find it hard to say 'accident' 'bout somebody what didn' volunteer for hauling logs in the first place." Mae Mae stared hard at Mark, gauging how he would react to her last statement. Seeing nothing but sympathy in his eyes, she went on.

"Now, Uncle Gee and his mama, they lived on another place. The white man what owned them was a good man. When my granddaddy—tha's Uncle Gee's daddy—died, the white man, he got ahold of this thing"—she indicated the item in Mark's hand—"and sometime . . . when he was two or three years old, the white man put it 'round the neck of that little child, Uncle Gee. When Gee growed up a bit, the man told him that he figured this thing to be special. Said it was only for Uncle Gee. The man said it was a gift from a daddy to his boy."

Dorry took the object from Mark and compared the two again. "Mae Mae, did your Uncle Gee call this a food stone?"

"Yes, he did," she said. "He said it was his inspiration."

Mark scooted to the edge of the couch and leaned forward a bit. "Why do you suppose he called it that—a food stone?"

"'Cause tha's what it was." She turned to Dorry. "This boy ain't been listening to my story." They all chuckled at Mae Mae's pretended exasperation. Then, to Mark, she continued, "Ever'body knew it was a food stone. It's just somethin' ever'body knew. Or at least *used* to know. Now I'm talkin' 'bout my people, you hear?

"That plantation my granddaddy worked, it was 'posed to been some fine place. When he got killed, the whole thing just fell apart. Crops didn't yield. Weeds took over. White folk said it was on account of the weather, but Mama said the slaves knew it was cause they lost the food stone."

"What happened when your uncle got it?"

"Jus' what you thinkin' happened," she said smugly. "The plantation Gee was on bloomed like the Garden of Eden. All the black folk on that place was so excited that the food stone had come to one of their own . . . on account of they knew what it meant. The white man, he didn't put no stock in it, but the black folk knew they'd be eatin' from the excess, and they was happy! Tha's the story my mama always told anyhow. And from that day, anybody with the stone, they got a green thumb like you ain't never seen."

"You said Uncle Gee wore this," Mark said. "Did he have a green thumb when he grew up?"

For a moment, Mae Mae paused. With virtually no expression on her face, she stared at Mark, then said simply, "Yes."

"Do you . . . or did he . . ." Dorry tried to find the correct words. "Did anyone ever tell you this was script? Writing?"

"I ain't never talked to nobody about it. And Uncle Gee never said, if he knew. But I figured it was some kinda writin'—all them marks on the side."

At that point, Dorry told her about the translation of the

object that had been found in their backyard. She pointed out her observation that the etchings on her "food stone" were identical except for a small section. While Mae Mae retrieved a large magnifying glass from her bedroom, Dorry arranged the two objects side by side on the ottoman. For the rest of the morning, they talked and examined the pieces of the past that had brought them into each others' company. Dorry related Dylan's analysis to Mae Mae and the chemical conclusion of leaded bronze. She was astonished to learn, after all these years, that her "food stone" wasn't a stone at all.

Mark drew an exact copy of the script from the "food stone" on paper and went outside to fetch his cell phone from the rental car. He intended to track down Dylan and see about faxing the copy to him in hopes of having it quickly translated.

When he returned, Mark reported that he had indeed reached their friend at a restaurant in Los Angeles.

"Abby is out there too. He gave me the number of their hotel so we can fax this to them." He brandished the page. "But they're at a convention and it'll be about three hours before she's out of her session so . . ." He shrugged.

"You wanna go to lunch?" Dorry said to Mae Mae.

"To a restaurant?" she asked.

"Yes, ma'am."

"Lord, jus' let me get my coat!" Mae Mae laughed. "Say, can we go to the bakery downtown?"

"Just show us the way!" Mark grinned.

On their way out the door, Mae Mae said, "Help me down the steps, boy," to Mark and then exclaimed, "Look here at Mae Mae's garden. Uncle Gee wadn' the only one wif a green thumb!" As they walked around the side of the house, Mark and Dorry oohed and aahed while the proud old lady pointed out her obvious success with virtually everything she planted.

A few minutes later, they were almost to the car when Mae Mae suddenly stopped. Thinking something was wrong, Mark and Dorry stopped too. "Are you okay, Mae Mae?" Dorry asked.

"Oh, yes, baby girl," she replied. "I am fine as I can be." Then she cocked her head, popped her dentures forward and back one quick time, and said, "But I jus' had me a thought." She grinned. "All the talkin' we been doin', and you ain't nevah asked me what Uncle Gee's *real* name was. The man was famous."

And with that, she said, "Now, help Mae Mae in the car."

⚛ SIX

MISSOURI—JANUARY 1865

MOSES HAD BEEN SITTING IN THE WAGON FOR
well over an hour and was thankful there was no wind. It
was cold enough without the wind, he thought. He could
see clearly by the soft luminescence of the stars and a rising
moon. He studied the breath as it rushed from his nostrils. It
reminded him of fire from dragons in the books he read to
the children at the farm. Eerily, he noticed, the vapor didn't
rise or fall, but drifted in a flat line across the back of the dun
mare in front of him. Moses had hitched her to his buckboard early that evening, but didn't leave home until after
ten o'clock that night. It had taken him three hours or so
to make it to this particular crossroad on the Kansas border.

He had worn two coats over several shirts and was too
numb to remember how many pairs of pants he had put
on. The boots weren't helping much, nor was the quilt he
had wrapped around his head. He had been told, "No fire,"
and he knew the reason, but was mad that he had not been
told how long he'd have to wait. He was mad . . . and scared.

The wagon jerked. "Whoa. Whoa now," he said soothingly as he turned to calm the stallion tied to the back corner. The big, black horse was a legend, instantly recognizable
to anyone from Diamond Grove all the way to Springfield.
He was a racer and had earned the man quite a sum of
money the last few years. Even during the midst of the war,
people came out to see him run. The stallion had never lost
a race.

After four years of chaos, the horse was the only thing
he and his wife had left of any tangible value. Oh, there was
the land, of course, some working stock, and the house, but
there was no cash. The horse was the only thing he had
left—and that's just what they had demanded.

Moses eased to the edge of his seat and slid awkwardly
to the frozen ground. He walked carefully to the back of
the wagon, speaking in low tones, seeking to still the huge
animal. For a moment, he stood close and bathed in the
warm clouds of breath as the horse blew and stamped a
foot nervously.

The trace chains on the mare rattled as she shook.
Moses saw that the old plow horse had turned her head to
the left and held her ears straight up. Then, she nickered,
sending more shivers down the man's already frozen spine.
It was a high-pitched sound, drawn out and punctuated by
a snort that cut through the frigid night like an arrow.

He eased away from the stallion and carefully inched up
beside the mare, watching in the direction she indicated
and straining to see through the darkness. He heard the
riders before he saw them—could hear the horses they
rode breaking the ice in frozen puddles. When the first of
the four men came into view, he began to murmur a Bible
verse his mother had taught him as a boy.

"I will fear no evil: for thou art with me . . ."

As the riders lined up in front of the wagon, his heart felt as though it might come out of his chest. They wore cloth sacks fitted snugly to their heads. The sacks were tied at the neck with holes cut for the eyes. Each of the men was covered in a sheet, his head pushed through a hole in the middle, causing the white material to flow over him like a robe. Three of the men held Navy Colt pistols while the leader—the first man he had seen—carried a forty-caliber Henry carbine. It was a short, ugly weapon known for its accuracy and effectiveness.

They were "night riders"—a part of Quantrill's Raiders— men who used the war as an excuse to terrorize the border states of Missouri and Kansas. When William Clarke Quantrill formed his band of three hundred men in late 1861, they were quickly acknowledged by Confederates, Unionists, and civilians alike as butchers who were on no one's side but their own.

Quantrill actively recruited psychopaths such as "Bloody Bill" Anderson, his lieutenant, who participated in raids wearing scalps around his neck. The Youngers—Jim, Bob, and Cole—were a part of this group, as were Frank and Jesse James. On August 21, 1863, they rode into Lawrence, Kansas, burned every building, robbed both banks, and murdered 183 unarmed men and boys—most in front of their families.

The leader of the four riders spoke. "Moses? How's Susan?"

Suddenly weak in the knees, the man felt raw fear as a sickening comprehension swept over him.

"Still ain't got no kids, do ya?" When the man only blinked, the leader screamed, "I said, 'Do ya?'!"

"No. We don't," Moses replied.

As soon as he received an answer, the rider assumed a friendly voice. "Well, that's too bad," he said. "Maybe Susan needs a real man. I 'specially like her blond hair. Don't you?" Again expecting a reply, he raised his voice. "Don't you?"

"Yes."

Moses stood there and took it. His mouth was awash with the hot, acid saliva that accompanies nausea, but he didn't dare move or even spit. He knew what they were doing. The men were letting him know that they knew everything about him and his wife. It was a threat, plain and simple.

Moses and his wife, Susan, were slave-owning Union sympathizers whose home and farm—even before the war—had become a haven for slaves. It was well known that Moses spent his money on slaves only to free them immediately. Of course, the blacks stayed on and others joined them because, in that place, they were not mistreated.

A week earlier to the day marked the third time Moses' farm had been hit by a group of Quantrill's men. They came at night, in packs, like wild dogs, tearing at everything in their path. So far, no one on his place had been hurt or killed. But during this last attack, Mary, a black woman who helped his wife in the house and had become her friend, had been taken, along with Mary's infant child.

When the Quantrill men had ridden onto his property the week before, they had come early in the evening, just after dark. Mary's other son, James, was inside the house with Susan and Moses, but Mary had been outside nursing the baby. She was in the swing under the oak tree when they swept in. The riders had fired guns into the air and more than one had swung a torch into the loft of the barn.

Fortunately, several families of freed slaves were living in the barn and they quickly extinguished the blaze. But when the raiders were gone and order restored, Mary and her baby boy were missing.

Susan had been inconsolable, and yet there was literally nothing to be done. One dared not complain to the law. Moses knew that his own sheriff might well be one of the riders who sat before him at this very moment. The same was true of his preacher, doctor, and blacksmith. Ordinary men with ordinary lives, who might otherwise greet a person in the daylight with a wave or even a kind word, often harbored in their minds a hatred and violence only unleashed after dark. He was well aware that only two years before, Quantrill himself had been a schoolteacher.

Yesterday, a message had come to Moses through a neighbor who said he had been ordered to convey specific instructions to his friend. These instructions included the location and approximate time of a meeting, if he so desired, with a group of Quantrill's men. There was an impolite suggestion that his stallion might be traded for the lives of Mary and her child.

A match flared as the rider on the right lit the stump of a cigar. Moses sensed the men winding down, their jokes and threats diminishing as they grew cold from lack of movement. He addressed the leader. "I don't see Mary or the baby. I brought the stallion."

The man urged his horse forward aggressively. "We decided she didn't get to make this trip," he said. One of the men snickered. The leader ordered the rider with the cigar to untie the stallion, which he moved immediately to do. Moses spun about, intending to protest, when he heard the carbine cock. "Stay right where you are, Moses," he heard and slowly turned to find the Henry aimed at his face.

The leader shifted in his saddle as he pointed the rifle with one hand. "You got the hoss?" he said to the man at the back of the wagon.

"Got 'im," Moses heard behind him.

Moses swallowed hard as the leader, still holding the carbine with one hand, extended it closer to his face. "I'm thinkin' I can kill you or you can walk," the man said. "You want to walk?"

Moses nodded weakly.

The man paused and appeared to think for a moment, then asked, "You boys like Moses?" The others grunted affirmations that, yes indeed, they did like Moses, and the leader, seemingly having made up his mind as well, agreed. "I like him too," the man said as he appeared to relax. "So, Moses . . . you get to walk."

With those words, the man swung the rifle away from Moses, placed the barrel directly between the eyes of the old mare, and pulled the trigger. The forty-caliber blast from the Henry was deafening. Instantly, the mare went down in her harness and pulled the buckboard over on its side. In her death throes, the horse sprayed tissue and blood onto Moses as he got to his knees and held her head in shock.

The stallion added to the general panic as the rider's mounts reacted to the sudden shot and the sounds of the dying mare. But cutting through the din, Moses heard the frightened screams of a baby. Looking up, he saw the man with the rifle struggling to control his horse as he untied a burlap sack from the saddle. Succeeding, he held the bag aloft and said, "He ain't dead." Then, he wheeled his horse and added, "Here's your trade," as he slung the bag in the direction of Moses.

"Oh, Jesus!" Moses cried out as he leaped from his knees to catch the bag. "Oh, Jesus, please."

He was vaguely conscious of the thundering of hooves as the riders galloped away. Quickly, but with infinite care, Moses placed the bag onto the dead mare and cut away the cord that bound the opening. Pulling the stiff burlap from around the crying child, he could see that someone had wrapped him in a piece of blanket before tying the bag. It was the only reason the baby was still alive.

As Moses lifted the sobbing infant, he could see by the light of the moon that the baby boy was ashen and moving with difficulty. Moses ripped his gloves off. With his bare hands, he could feel the naked child's icy skin. He clawed desperately at the buttons on his coats and the shirts underneath, finally tearing them open to create a warm spot for the infant.

Settling the still frantic child against the skin of his belly and refastening the clothes around him, Moses lurched to his feet and, without delay, began to walk back in the direction from which he had come. He knew better than to stay and build a fire. The problem, as he saw it, was nourishment. He could keep the baby warm, but this child needed milk and, of course, he had none. There had been a homestead several miles back. Surely, they would help.

Moses' pace calmed the baby. Walking swiftly through the frigid darkness, he talked softly to the child and soon sensed him drifting into an uneasy sleep. He was sad about Mary. She was dead. Of that, he was certain. Moses didn't look forward to returning to his wife without her friend, but at least he had managed to rescue a part of Mary.

He looked at the moon and said a prayer as he trudged across the frozen ground. He and Susan would raise this boy as their own—Susan would insist on it. *And*, he thought, *I'll give the boy my name. We'll just add "Carver" to the name Mary already gave him.*

He smiled, remembering the laughter they'd all shared when Mary had named her baby after a president. "That's a long name for a tiny boy!" he had told her.

Gonna be a longer name now, Moses thought. Then, as he walked, Moses patted the sleeping child whose life was beginning without a flicker of promise and spoke his name aloud. "George Washington Carver."

Iowa—September 1895

It was midmorning on a Saturday and already promising to be a hot day. Henry Wallace, a skinny, dark-haired boy with bright blue eyes and a friendly personality, was excited to be with George Washington Carver again. Henry was a chatterbox who never seemed to run out of questions for his older friend.

"Let's not get too close to the water now," the slender black man said to the rambunctious seven-year-old. "Your daddy would have a fit if I let you get eaten by a hippopotamus."

The little boy laughed. "Oh, George!" Henry said. "There aren't any hippopotamuses here!"

"If you say so," George replied as he peered over the child's shoulder. "But I don't like crocodiles either, so just do me a favor and stay away from the lake."

Frequently, Henry's father, a dairy science professor at

Iowa State University, allowed his son to accompany the brilliant student on one of his "botanical expeditions." Together, the small white boy and the young man with jet-black skin made an interesting pair as they traversed the forests and fields surrounding the campus.

Soon after arriving at Iowa State, George had distinguished himself as a scholar. During the years of his undergraduate work, he had amassed quite a collection of local plant life and his agricultural work already rivaled that of his teachers. Professor Wallace saw the polite, well-spoken graduate student as an excellent companion for his young son and encouraged their time together. He knew something of George's long struggle for an education and considered little Henry fortunate to have the opportunity to learn from a man so hungry for knowledge.

George was thirty years old and about to complete his pursuit of a master's degree in botany. As a child he had learned to read and write at home on the Carver farm, and at the age of twelve had been given permission to move to Neosho to begin formal schooling. Moses and Susan, his surrogate parents, had been sad to see him leave, but knew that his thirst for learning was far beyond that which they were able to quench.

So Moses had arranged for George to live with Andrew and Mariah Watkins as he attended the Lincoln School for Negro Children. Two years later, having reached a point where his knowledge exceeded that of his teacher, George moved to Fort Scott, and then on to Minneapolis, Kansas, where he finished the equivalent of high school.

Soon George was awarded an academic scholarship to Highland University.

From the time George had lived with the Watkins family, he had worked as a cook and housekeeper—even managing to save a bit of money from his meager wages. He was therefore able to afford the trip to Kansas by wagon. All seemed in order—the correspondence and registration had been completed by mail—until George arrived at Highland. The president of the university saw him and indignantly demanded, "Why didn't you tell me you were a Negro?" and literally slammed the door in his face.

Throughout the next several years, George had experienced that same reaction many different times, until finally, he had been accepted (and admitted) to Simpson College in Indianola, Iowa. There he excelled, later transferring to Iowa State where he studied bacteriology, entomology, chemistry, and zoology, in addition to his courses in botany. George Carver had completed his undergraduate work with honors and quickly set his sights on a graduate degree. Now, with a master's degree in botany about to be earned, he had become well known among the faculty as one who would soon join their ranks. George was loved and well respected.

"What is this one?" the little boy asked loudly. He was indicating a plant growing beside a fence post.

George ambled over, a sly grin on his face. When he answered, he spoke in a high-pitched, raspy voice—leftover evidence of a childhood bout with whooping cough. "Well, smell it, Henry. Go on, now, take you a good, deep whiff."

The boy leaned over and inhaled through his nose. Immediately, he was seized by an uncontrollable bout of sneezing and laughter. Finally, he wiped his nose on his arm and rubbed his eyes with the knuckles of his small fists. Still giggling, he said, "I knew it was ragweed!"

"And I knew you knew it," George said. "You just like to sneeze your head off! So, Mr. Smartypants, do you remember the Latin name for ragweed?"

Henry Wallace closed one eye and tilted his head back. With one hand out in front of him as if he were trying to pluck the words from his memory, he said, "Ahhhmmm . . . ohhhhhh . . . shoot! *Ambrosia* something?"

"That's right. Do you remember the rest of it?"

The boy screwed up his face again, but came up empty. "I don't," he said. "Tell me one more time."

"*Ambrosia artemisiifolia.*"

"Right! *Artemisiifolia. Ambrosia artemisiifolia!* I got it!"

"I'm sure you do," George said. "Now let's get moving. We have a lot of ground to cover."

After several hours, George gestured toward a huge oak tree on the bank of a stream and said, "You ready for a sandwich? I'm hungry. I hope you can tell me the formal name of those dandelions over there—because that's the password that unlocks *your* bag of food!"

"*Taraxacum officinale,*" the boy said at once. Then, placing his hand on the black man's arm, added, "And . . . it is edible and medicinal."

George chuckled as he turned and headed for the shade of the big tree. "Lord! You buckin' for a bite of *my* sandwich!"

In the shadow of the green canopy, they took off their shoes and shirts and, dangling their feet in the cool, shallow water of the stream, unwrapped a simple lunch. "Let me see . . . ," George said. "You want a cheese sandwich—or a cheese sandwich?"

"Cheese," Henry grinned.

They ate in silence for several moments, enjoying the comfort of this place they'd found. The leafy ceiling invited a breeze through their natural dining room that gently cooled them as they rested. Soon though, Henry was asking questions about every green thing within reach. George had grown to love the child and was proud that Henry's father trusted him with the boy. It was a responsibility that he did not take lightly, and he relished his role as a mentor.

"George?" the boy asked. "Where did you get the food stone?"

George sighed. "Henry, you have heard that story a thousand times."

"I know," the boy said excitedly, "but I like to hear it. Please, can I wear it again while you tell me?"

"*May* I . . ."

"*May* I wear it again while you tell me? Please?"

"Okay," George said resignedly as he pulled the leather cord attached to the oddly shaped object from around his neck. Before placing it over the head of the child, George asked a question. "Henry, do you pledge to do something special with your life?"

"I do," the boy nodded solemnly.

"Then here you go." George put the strange necklace on the child and began to speak. It was a simple story, and having told it to the boy so many times, he attempted an abbreviated version. "My daddy wore the food stone—"

"In Africa," Henry interrupted.

"Yes, in Africa. He wore the food stone in Africa. Then, when he was brought here—"

"He still had it and he always wore it and nobody took it from him," the boy said in a rush.

George opened his eyes wide and turned his head to look directly at the boy. "And then when . . ." He waited.

Henry spoke instantly. "And then when your real daddy was killed, your other daddy, Mr. Carver, got the food stone and gave it to you. And he gave it to you because he said you were created for something special and that the food stone was a gift from a father to his son."

George stared at Henry for a moment, then spoke. "Do you like it when I tell you that story?"

The boy answered, "I do," and they lay back on the ground and laughed.

For a time, the two rested there in the grass beside the stream. George had rolled over onto his stomach and was examining a tiny patch of watercress growing on the bank. Meanwhile Henry had stayed on his back and, with the cord still around his neck, was deep in concentration as he held the food stone close to his face. "How long have you worn it?" he asked.

George tossed a pebble into the water. "Since I was a baby, I suppose. Truth is, I don't recall *not* wearing it."

"Why *do* you wear it though?"

George swiveled onto his side and propped his head with a hand. "Because it came from my father," he said. "My daddy wore it his whole life, and though I never knew him, I suspect he was a special man."

Henry seemed to consider this, then asked, "Was he a special man because he wore the food stone?"

"No, child," George said carefully. "He was a special man because he decided to be."

"George?" The child moved to a sitting position facing his friend. His legs were crossed "Indian style" as he leaned forward with the object and indicated the markings on one side. "Do you know what this says?"

"Yes," George replied. "It says, 'Henry Wallace will be a

great man. His life will make a difference in this world, because he will always choose to make a difference.'"

"Wow! Really?" Henry asked.

"That's it," George said. "That stone you hold says the same thing to me. It represents my father reminding me every day that I am important—that I have a mission in my life."

"What is your mission?"

"Henry, my mission is to learn to do common things uncommonly well and to use those skills and that knowledge to change the lives of those less fortunate than myself. And I'm going to do that with plants. People're starving, child, and anything that helps fill the dinner pail is valuable."

"That's my mission too," the boy said earnestly. "Will you help me?"

"Of course," George responded. "As you grow up, remember that you have worn the food stone and pledged to do something special with your life. You won't always have George around, but that won't matter. Because *you* have been made to make a difference. And I believe that you will."

❧ SEVEN

THE AIR WAS THICK. THE TWO MEN, FACING EACH other with only a desk between them, talked in harsh whispers. At two o'clock in the afternoon, the thermometer outside the administration building had reached 102 degrees; however, it wasn't the heat or humidity in the president's office that had negatively affected the atmosphere. The tension, on this day, not only trumped the heat but created a climate of intensity that was quickly becoming unbearable.

When Booker Taliaferro Washington had arrived to take the helm of Tuskegee Institute in 1881, he had no buildings, no students, and no teachers. In a few short years, starting with an appropriation of just two thousand dollars from the Alabama State Legislature, he had created the premier black educational establishment in the nation. Luring the brilliant, but infuriating, man who now sat before him to the campus as a teacher had been one of his greatest successes and a primary reason for the school's considerable growth.

In April of 1896, George Carver, then a professor at Iowa State and already reputed to be a scientific prodigy of immense proportions, received an interesting offer from the renowned educator. In his letter, Dr. Washington wrote, "I cannot offer you money, position, or fame. The first two you have. The last, from the position you now occupy, you will no doubt achieve. These things I now ask you to give up. I offer you in their place: work—hard, hard work, the task of bringing a people from degradation, poverty, and waste to full manhood. Your department exists only on paper and your laboratory will have to be in your head."

Carver's acceptance was immediate, and after fulfilling his obligations at Iowa State, he turned his attention to Dr. Washington's challenge. He arrived at the rail station in Chehaw, Alabama, in early October and was taken to the campus in Tuskegee by wagon. There, the professor unpacked his microscope, assorted chemicals, and his one suit. Dr. Washington had personally escorted him to the one-room apartment he would call home, watching closely for any sign that his newest faculty member might suddenly change his mind and flee. But, of course, there was none.

Through the course of several years, Professor Carver's classes—which included botany, chemistry, and soil study—evolved into the Department of Scientific Agriculture. The teacher became an inventor, creating new varieties of plants and fertilizers. He taught farmers and their families how to preserve foods for the winter and produced recipes and menus that introduced balanced diets and increased vitality to the poor.

It was Carver's latest discovery, however, that had now embroiled Tuskegee Institute in controversy and convinced Dr. Booker T. Washington that the school was in trouble.

The fifty-eight-year-old Washington perspired profusely as he tried to ignore the afternoon heat. He leaned forward and spoke to the most admired member of his faculty.

"Professor Carver . . . George . . . what have we done?"

"Well, Dr. Washington," Carver answered in his high, raspy voice, "I don't think *we* have done anything. You are certainly not to blame for any consternation on the part of the farmers. It seems that this is entirely my doing." George clasped his hands in his lap, not nervously, for he wasn't nervous, but in the manner of one exhibiting extreme patience.

The president shook his head. "It's not just our people, George. The white farmers are afraid too." He glanced around and lowered his voice even more. "We're receiving threats. You . . . and the school. And the State Agricultural Board is sending an investigative delegation tomorrow morning. George—they could shut us down." He rubbed his face with his hands. "My Lord . . . I never saw this coming . . . I have been traveling so much . . ." Drawing a deep breath, he said, "Take me back to the beginning here. Maybe we can figure out what to do. Why in the world did they plant so many peanuts in the first place?"

"Dr. Washington, you know I appreciate the level of trust you've placed in me over the years." George wiped his brow. "You've never second-guessed me or watched over my shoulder. And you know that I've always had the best interest of the farmer in mind—even when I'm dealing with the students." Washington nodded patiently. "But that degree of trust has naturally placed you in a position of being somewhat uninformed in regards to my daily efforts. Do you remember that barren twenty-one-acre tract on the east boundary of campus? It was donated to the school four years ago."

"Yes, I remember," Washington replied. "It was given to us because it was worthless."

"That's right," George confirmed. "I checked the county records. The last planting of cotton, it produced forty-four pounds per acre. That was four years ago—the soil was worn out. On a small scale, I had been experimenting with naturally produced fertilizer for some time. This, I saw, was an opportunity to step up the research."

As George took a breath, the president broke in. "Naturally produced fertilizer? I'm not following you . . . and are we getting to the peanuts?"

George cleared his throat. "Yes, Dr. Washington, we are. Most fertilizer has, as its basis, nitrogen. Legumes—plants like cow peas and peanuts—are plants that have nitrogen-producing bacteria on their roots. Simply explained, the bacteria removes nitrogen from the air and distributes it through the root system into the soil, which becomes enriched."

"So, am I to assume that you planted peanuts on that barren plot?"

"Yes, sir. Peanuts. For two years we planted peanuts. The third year, we planted that same twenty-one acres in cotton again." George paused and watched the president of the college, waiting for the question he knew would come.

"And?" Dr. Washington drew out the word, a hint of exasperation creeping into his voice.

"And, in the third year, that twenty-one-acre parcel of land produced almost eleven thousand pounds of cotton. By the way, the math on that works out to more than five hundred pounds of cotton per acre."

Dr. Washington was incredulous. Leaning forward, he looked around quickly as if to conceal a secret and said, "Does anyone else know about this?"

"Of course!" Carver exclaimed. "I made certain that every farmer between Montgomery and Columbus saw the field with their own eyes. That's why they planted the peanuts!"

Dr. Washington fell back in his chair and exhaled. He peered out the window and nervously rapped his knuckles on the desk. Then he stood and, walking around the desk to George, sat on its corner and said, "I want to make sure I have this straight. You convinced every farmer within a hundred miles of here to plant peanuts because their soil was worn out."

"The soil *was* worn out," George insisted. "It was—"

Dr. Washington held up his hand. "Let me finish," he said. He took a deep breath to compose himself and continued. "Long story short, these men planted all their fields in peanuts. Now they have thousands of pounds— tons—of peanuts, and there is no market for their crop. Is that correct?"

"At this moment, yes," Carver responded. "That is correct."

The president stood and slammed his fist on the desk. Shoving his face into the face of the younger man, he growled, "Holy God, man! Do you not understand what this means to this university? These white farmers hold our very lives in their hands! We only exist because of the gracious favor of the state legislature, and now we have potentially ruined a third of the farming families in this state!"

"Dr. Washington," George said softly, "those farmers would have been ruined within the year in any case. People would have starved."

Washington slammed his hand down on the desk again and cursed. "But not by our hand!" he shouted. "They would not have starved by *our* hand!"

For several long moments, both men were silent. The
college president stalked around the office glowering at the
professor who continued to annoy him by remaining calm.
Before too long, however, George Carver spoke. When he
did, it was with a gentle voice. "Dr. Washington, I have
admired you for many years. From you, I have learned to
deal with the ups and downs of life. You told me when I
came here that 'character, not circumstances, makes the
man.' What we have here, sir, is a circumstance.

"You educated me about service to others. You said,
'The world cares very little about what a person knows. It's
what a person *does* with what he knows that counts.' Sir,
we are *doing*.

"I have learned about power from you. In your address
to our incoming students just last week, you said, 'There are
two ways of exerting one's strength: one is pushing down—
the other is pulling up.' I believe that we are pulling up."

As the president sat back down in his chair, George
Carver stood up. His voice grew stronger as he spoke.
"From you, sir, I have learned about the control that a lack
of self-image has upon our people. After publicly praising
a young farmer one day, you said privately to me, 'No race
can prosper until it learns that there is as much dignity in
tilling a field as in writing a poem.' Sir, surely you recognize the vast fields we are tilling."

Dr. Washington's lip began to quiver, but he held Carver's
gaze as now Carver circled the desk and leaned close to his
mentor's face. He continued. "Dr. Washington, you taught
me about white people and love and the capacity of my
own heart. Do you remember the day you and I called on
the state assemblyman in Montgomery? Do you remember
that, sir?"

"Yes," Washington said as his eyes pooled and a tear ran down his cheek.

George clasped the president's forearm with his hands as he sank to one knee beside the chair. "The assemblyman was in charge of textbook appropriations for every college in the state. After he smiled and told you 'no,' what did the man call you?" Dr. Washington was silent. His eyes slowly fell to his lap. "Sir," George repeated. "What did the man call you?"

"A nigger."

"A what?"

The president's head raised. With tears flowing freely, he looked George directly in the eye and said, "A nigger. The man called me a nigger."

"That's right, Dr. Washington. Then you walked out of his office and before we exited the building, you said to me and I quote: 'I will permit no man to narrow and degrade my soul by making me hate him.'

"Sir, you have shown me that there is value in adversity, that my challenges build muscle, and that my decisions matter. Let me deliver to you some powerful words that I have committed to memory. These are from page 197 of your autobiography." George closed his eyes and recited. "I have learned that success is to be measured not so much by the position that one has reached in life as by the obstacles he has overcome while choosing to succeed. Out of the hard and unusual struggle through which one is compelled to pass, he gets a strength and confidence that another might miss whose pathway is comparatively smooth by reason of birth or race."

Opening his eyes and standing, George said, "Dr. Booker T. Washington, I say to you that we are overcoming an obstacle far greater than an abundance of peanuts. You have shown me that we are one race—the human race. Color of skin and form of hair mean nothing, but length and width and breadth of soul mean everything. I love these farmers. And though, at the moment, they surely do not love me, I will find an answer for these good men. I feel certain that in the long run, what we are now experiencing will prove beneficial for the farmers and for our school."

Dr. Washington removed a handkerchief from his pocket, wiped his eyes, and blew his nose. "All right. I can accept that," he said, rising. "For now though . . . what do we do next? And what should I tell the Agricultural Board?"

George thought for a moment, then answered. "Most of the farmers are just beginning their harvest. I don't wish to frighten you, but their fear—and our situation—will get worse before it gets better. Tell the Ag Board that you will have an announcement in two weeks . . . no, make that ten days . . . an announcement about new uses and opportunities for the peanut. Urge them to be patient and tell them that the farmer with the largest crop of peanuts will be the happiest farmer when your announcement is made."

Dr. Washington's eyebrows lifted.

"And, sir," George continued with a mischievous smile, "give the Board this information with that sly look that says, 'I know something that I am not telling you.'"

The president shook his head and grinned wryly. "I *will* know something that I won't be telling them, George. I won't be telling them that I have no idea what I am talking about!"

George laughed.

"Seriously," Dr. Washington asked, "what are your plans?"

George lifted his chin. "I will be creating new uses and opportunities for the peanut."

Dr. Washington sighed patiently. "There is no need to remind you that there are only ten days to accomplish this feat. After all, you just gave me the timetable. But I am curious . . . how do you intend to create these new uses and opportunities?"

"Well, sir," George began, "the way I have it figured . . . I won't have to *create* anything. The uses and opportunities already exist for the peanut. I just don't know yet what they are. Now here's the thing . . ." He lowered his voice conspiratorially and moved closer to Dr. Washington. "All my life, I have risen regularly at four in the morning to go into the woods and talk with God. That's where He reveals His secrets to me. When everybody else is asleep, I hear God best and learn my plan. I never grope for methods. After my morning talk with Him, I go into the laboratory and carry out His wishes for the day. And this morning . . ." He glanced around. "This morning, I asked Him why He made the peanut."

The president just looked at him. Then, he opened his mouth as if to speak, but closed it again.

"Go on now," George urged with a chuckle. "Ask the question that's burning up the inside of your mouth."

"Okay, then," Dr. Washington responded, "what was God's answer?"

"First of all," George began, "I was out there in the dark feeling sorry for myself. I've already talked to some of the farmers who are upset, so I knew this situation was about to bust loose. Sometimes, when I get to feeling sorry for myself, I ask too much of the good Lord. And I did that very thing this morning. I said, 'God, why did You make the universe?' And He replied, 'George, you need to ask something more in proportion to that little mind of yours!'

So I said, 'Okay, Lord, then tell me why You made the world or why You made people.' He said, 'Sorry. Still far too much for your small brain.'

"But I kept pushing it. I asked, 'Why did You create plants?' The Lord answered, 'That is yet another subject beyond your meager powers of comprehension.'

"So, very meekly, I asked, 'The peanut?' and the Lord God said, 'Yes! For your modest level of intelligence, I will grant you the mysteries of the peanut. Take it inside your laboratory,' He told me, 'and separate the peanut into water, fats, oils, gums, resins, sugars, starches, and amino acids. Then recombine these under My three laws of compatibility, temperature, and pressure. Then,' the good Lord said, 'you will know why I made the peanut!'"

With those words, George spread his arms out wide and added, "And in ten days, Dr. Washington, we will have ourselves some answers!"

Both men laughed heartily, then the president asked, "Does God always provide you with answers?"

George leaned forward, suddenly serious again. "Let me put it this way: The Lord always provides me with life-changing ideas. Not that I am special. The Lord provides *everyone* with life-changing ideas. These ideas are quite literally a treasure map from the Almighty. It is up to each of us, however, to choose to dig for the treasure. Every man and woman on the planet contains within them the power to change the world, but this power is only manifested when one makes a conscious choice to use it."

George considered his words, then added, "This is why our world contains so many people who are depressed and unfulfilled. They have joined the growing multitudes who do not act upon the life-changing ideas that are theirs alone. A person who is *acting* upon an idea is happy and fulfilled. But a person who only *intends* to do this or that spirals into an ever-deepening pool of guilt and regret.

"Think of the books and songs that will never be written—works that will remain only in the mind of a person too fearful or selfish or lazy to dig for the treasure. And I am convinced—I have no proof of this, you understand, but I am convinced—that every choice one makes and every action one takes, or doesn't take, significantly affects the lives of everyone else. We are all connected to each other through our actions. Our decisions to act or not to act, to help or not to help—well, those choices create a ripple effect that can last for centuries.

"Here's what I mean. Take, for example, a person who has literally changed the world with an invention. Often, a person like that might point to a particular book that directed or inspired him to his life's work. Now, to whom do we owe the debt of gratitude for enriching our lives so significantly with that invention? The inventor? Or the author of the book that the inventor freely admits led him to a life of inventing in the first place?"

George shifted in his chair and, crossing his arms, tapped his chin with a forefinger as if lost in thought. "Or do we thank the teacher who encouraged the child to become an author? Certainly, without the teacher, the book would never have been written. And of course, this was the very book that inspired the person who created the invention that changed the world."

With his finger still tapping his chin, George watched Dr. Washington from the corner of his eye and continued to think out loud. "Or is the world indebted to the old woman who created a scholarship fund so that a young person could go to college and become the teacher who encouraged the child who became the author of the book that inspired the person whose invention changed the world? Maybe we owe our appreciation to the man who drove the wagon . . ." George paused.

Transfixed, Booker T. Washington—the man who himself had been a slave and whom many were already calling one of the greatest minds of the twentieth century—simply stared at his friend. Prompting George to finish his thought, he repeated his last words. "The man who drove the wagon?"

"You know, the man who drove the wagon . . . that carried the lumber that was used to build the doctor's office. Nobody ever knew! But the doctor's office was where the woman's life was saved who, several years later, bore the child who grew up to create the scholarship fund in the first place." He smiled and stood up. "Yes, we definitely need to thank the man who drove the wagon, because *he* is the one who changed the world."

With that, George shrugged and walked to the door. Before leaving, he turned one last time and said, "Or maybe somebody helped the man who drove the wagon, you think?" He smiled broadly, then added, "In any case, there's more going on in Tuskegee, Alabama, than a bunch of people with too many peanuts. That ain't the end of *this* story."

ALABAMA—JANUARY 1943

"And when he emerged from his laboratory," the speaker said in a clear voice, "on the morning of the tenth day, the uses and opportunities he had discovered for the peanut included glue; shaving cream; shampoo; soap; insecticide;

peanut butter, of course; axle grease; diesel fuel; linoleum"—
the vice president of the United States of America turned
a page of his notes—"nitroglycerin; insulation; bleach;
ink . . ."

Dr. Frederick Patterson, president of Tuskegee Institute,
crossed, and then uncrossed, his legs. Austin Curtiss, George
Carver's assistant, was seated beside him on the left edge of
the new platform which had been finished just that morning by the Student Government Association. Patterson was
slightly cool, but otherwise comfortable on this sunny,
winter morning. Scanning the audience for familiar faces,
he recognized more than a few, including Henry Ford and
his wife, who were sitting on the first row. He directed his
attention back to the vice president, who continued reading excerpts from a list of items that had eventually totaled
more than three hundred, ". . . meat tenderizer; cooking oil;
vinegar; evaporated milk . . ."

For three days now, Tuskegee had experienced a deluge
of people arriving by air, bus, train, car, wagon, and on foot.
From all over the world, literally thousands had braved the
dangers and inconvenience of travel during this terrible
time of a world at war. The small town had neither the
hotels nor the restaurants to care for the guests, most of
whom had come uninvited. Therefore, many of them had
simply waited patiently in the fields and streets, gathering
in groups to talk quietly or occasionally build a small fire
after dark by which to keep the January chill at bay.

Every church and school building in Macon County—
even the courthouse—had opened their doors to provide
temporary accommodations for the families who flooded
the tiny community. And they had all come to honor the
man whose remains now lay in the polished oak casket

placed carefully on a large table at the foot of the platform. At the age of seventy-seven, George Washington Carver had died in his sleep sometime during the evening of January 5.

The crowd, some seated, but most standing, represented the world's every age and race—for he had touched them all. There was a delegation from India sent by Mahatma Gandhi, who had sought Carver's advice on building and maintaining his country's agricultural system. Officials from Great Britain, Brazil, and Chile were in attendance. Even Joseph Stalin, who had solicited Carver's help in exploiting the vast expanse of land in Russia, sent a representative to convey his respect. At the moment, all were listening in amazement to the list that punctuated a story they had heard many times.

". . . charcoal; textile dyes; wood stains; cosmetics; fertilizer; baby cream; tannic acid—and a sauce, butter substitute, and condiment that have become better known as Worcestershire, margarine, and mayonnaise." The vice president deliberately set the list aside and looked up. He was a slim man of average height. His silver hair matched the dark-gray suit he wore. Pinned on his lapel was a small cutting of spruce. From his vantage point on the platform, he could see that many others in the crowd had also attached a piece of greenery to a jacket or dress as a way of honoring the man whose life had counted for so much.

Removing his reading glasses, the vice president said, "As you may or may not know, I served this country as the secretary of agriculture for seven years. I have been in the unique position of being able to see firsthand the impact of Dr. Carver's work. Every day, I think about the hundreds of thousands of children whose lives have been saved in West Africa due to the protein available to them now in the form of peanut milk, which *he* taught the world to synthesize.

"He has made a difference in the war effort as well. Just last year, Dr. Carver authored an article that has evidently been printed and reprinted in every newspaper in America. You know the name of it." The audience was nodding and smiling. "Nature's Garden for Victory and Peace. Did you know that last summer, there were over twenty million victory gardens planted in our country?" There was an audible gasp from the crowd. "Statistics from the Department of Agriculture show that over 40 percent of the food consumed in our country this year will have been produced in victory gardens."

Austin Curtiss, Carver's assistant, began to applaud. He was only twenty years old and had never seen anyone clap at a funeral before, but to his way of thinking, it was entirely appropriate. Dr. Carver had taken him under his wing as an assistant and had changed the boy's life. Austin stood up . . . and for the barest of seconds thought he might applaud right by himself. But Dr. Patterson stood as well, as did every man, woman, and child in attendance, clapping and nodding their heads in approval.

When at last they sat down, the university president briefly put his arm around the young man's shoulders as the vice president continued. "Dr. Carver was a treasured individual to many of us here. Calvin Coolidge considered him a friend, as did Theodore Roosevelt and, of course, our current president, Franklin Delano Roosevelt. Harvey Firestone, Thomas Edison, and you, Mr. Ford . . ." He indicated the renowned industrialist on the front row. "All you men regarded Dr. Carver as an intimate friend, did you not?" Ford bobbed his head vigorously to indicate agreement.

The vice president leaned forward on the podium. The

ovation of a few moments before had somehow shifted the mood of this gathering from its somber beginnings to a more relaxed—almost celebratory—atmosphere. "Mr. Ford? I am curious," he said with a wink. "Were you ever able to convince Dr. Carver to accept any of your money?" Ford shook his head and mouthed the word *no* as he took his wife's hand and listened expectantly.

"I didn't think so," the vice president said. "And what did he *do* for you and Mr. Firestone?" Answering his own question, he continued to speak to Ford. "Amazingly, the man developed a plastic material from soybeans that you were able to use in your automobiles." Taking the whole audience in his gaze, he said, "And in a piece of science that astounds me to this day, Dr. Carver created a process of extracting rubber from the milk of the goldenrod plant." He paused, pivoted to shake his head in wonder at the two men seated on the platform behind him, then, as if in disbelief, repeated himself, "Rubber! . . . from the milk of the goldenrod plant."

The vice president paused and, lifting his head, spoke directly to a woman seated on the first row beside Henry Ford's wife. "Mrs. Bounds, would you join me on stage?" Then, he turned to the men seated behind him and added, "Dr. Patterson? Mr. Curtiss? Would you also join us here at the podium?"

The audience watched curiously as the vice president moved to the steps and extended his hand to a beautiful woman who appeared to be in her early forties. She had smooth, caramel-colored skin and wore a simple black dress. Helping her onto the platform, he spoke privately to her for a moment, then addressed the crowd. "You already know these two gentlemen. The lady who has joined us is

Mrs. Bonnie Mae Bounds from Fordyce, Arkansas. She is Dr. Carver's niece and only living relative."

As the vice president spoke, Dr. Patterson and Austin greeted Mrs. Bounds. Then all three directed their attention back to him. "Early this morning," he said, "I had the opportunity to read Dr. Carver's last will and testament. It was written on a single page of paper and in Dr. Carver's own hand. While I will admit, it is unusual to reveal the contents of a man's will at his burial, by the powers vested in me as an official representative of the United States government, I intend to do just that." A murmur ran through the crowd as the vice president held his hands up in a motion to request patience and quiet.

"There are only two provisions in the will. One is for Dr. Carver's financial estate. Now, one might rightly ask, 'How much could his financial estate possibly be?' After all, we are talking about a man who never took a raise or a single payment for outside work." He paused, looking over the audience whose attention was rapt. "So, how much did he *earn*? Quickly doing the math, one sees that during a term of forty-seven years and four months, Dr. Carver received 568 checks—each for exactly $125. That is a total gross earnings of $71,000.

"From this amount, Dr. Carver gave to his church, paid his bills, helped the less fortunate, and saved what he could manage." He turned to the university president. "Dr. Patterson? Dr. Carver wished to leave his estate to Tuskegee Institute. The savings, sir . . . money Dr. Carver would not spend on himself . . . total a bit more than sixty thousand dollars." There was a gasp from the crowd. Tears quickly became evident on the faces of many as Dr. Patterson shook his head and said softly, "Thank You, Lord."

The vice president continued to speak. "The second provision in Dr. Carver's will"—he paused—"was for this." He held up an item that tumbled from his hand and dangled at the end of a leather cord, swinging in the winter sunlight, holding the attention of every person present. "Dr. Carver wore this around his neck. It was his father's before him, who also wore it around *his* neck."

The vice president focused his gaze upon the lady. "Mrs. Bounds, Dr. Carver wanted you to have this." He moved to the small woman and, in full view of everyone, talked quietly to her for a moment. Then, as she bowed her head, he carefully placed the object around her neck.

The worn leather of the cord was smooth and cool against the bare skin of her neck as Bonnie Mae Bounds held her Uncle Gee's food stone in her hands. She had not seen it since she was a little girl—he had worn it under his shirt—but now she looked at its shape and color, running a fingertip across the rough grooves as she listened to the vice president's final words.

"Today, we bury this wonderful man next to his friend, Dr. Booker T. Washington, and we will miss him. He began each day with an earnest prayer that God would reveal to him the secrets of the flowers, plants, soil, and weeds. He wanted only to put more food in the bellies of the hungry, more clothing on the backs of the naked, and better shelter over the heads of the homeless. His work is now done. But because he has shown us the way . . . ours is just beginning."

WHEN THE VICE PRESIDENT HAD FINISHED THAT morning, he shook hands with Austin Curtiss, Dr. Patterson, and Bonnie Mae and descended the steps to speak momentarily with the Fords. Finally, he stopped at the coffin and bowed his head briefly before being escorted to his car and driven away.

Bonnie Mae had gone back to her seat beside Mrs. Ford and listened patiently as Dr. Patterson made his remarks and offered a final prayer. Afterward, the Fords had spoken to her—along with maybe a thousand other people who wanted only to hug her, shake her hand, or offer their condolences. She and her husband had not been alone for a single moment until they boarded the bus to begin the long journey back to Arkansas.

Falling asleep almost immediately, she had not awakened until the bus was well into Mississippi. It was dark when she opened her eyes. She felt first for the object around her neck, then spoke quietly. "Jerold? You awake?"

"Yes, girl," her husband answered. "I been awake. But you was some kind of tired."

"I'm still wore out," she said as she looked out the bus window. They were traveling on a rural highway, and occasionally, Bonnie Mae caught sight of a flickering fireplace shining through the cloth-covered window of some tiny farmhouse. *Those are the kind of people he helped,* she thought. "It's just all so sad, Jerold. Uncle Gee was the last of my people."

"I know, baby," he said to his wife, "but you can sure be proud. You heard the man today . . . right there in yo' Uncle Gee's house. Uncle Gee changed the world! Tha's what the man said!" Then, as an afterthought, wanting to cheer her up, Jerold added, "And you done met the vice president of the United States!"

She sat up straighter. "Yes, I did," she said. "And he

couldn'ta been nicer. When we was in Uncle Gee's place with him today—me an' the Curtiss boy—he told us all about growing up in Iowa. Did you know that his daddy taught Uncle Gee at college? And Uncle Gee took vice president Wallace all through the woods when he was a child. He said they collected plants together!" She was quiet for a moment, seemingly lost in thought, then said, "Do you know he told us to call him 'Henry'? We didn't do it, but he told us to!"

"Bonnie Mae," Jerold said, shifting in the uncomfortable bus seat to face his wife. "Bonnie Mae, what did the vice president say to you today? What did the man say right in front of ever'body when he gave you Uncle Gee's food stone?"

Her eyes brightened. "Oh, Lord," she said. "I almost forgot. He was so nice. Right before he put it around my neck, he said to me, he said, 'Bonnie Mae . . . do you pledge to do somethin' special with your life?'"

⽷ EIGHT

DURING THE RIDE TO LUNCH, THE CHANDLERS listened in stunned silence as Mae Mae told them the story of her Uncle Gee and how she came to possess the food stone. Sitting in the backseat, Dorry's journalistic instincts were "red-lining." She took notes and drew circles around the name Henry Wallace, intending to do an Internet search when she got home. Secretary of agriculture and vice president under Roosevelt? She had never heard of him.

It was ten minutes past noon as Mark held the door of Klappenbach's Bakery for Dorry and Mae Mae. Dorry commented later that she felt as though she were accompanying the queen of England when they entered the restaurant. The hostess escorted them directly to a booth—and several of the people standing by the door actually clapped as they passed. As they made their way across the restaurant, Mark was amused to see a wave of patrons stand to greet the town's most recognizable personality and call her by name. "Hey, Mae Mae!" a little girl yelled from the other side of the room.

Everyone laughed as the old woman yelled back, "Hey, Sugar! Get yo'sef over heah and give yo' Mae Mae a hug!" When the child did, the entire restaurant was watching and smiling.

Mark and Dorry were astonished. "It's kinda like being with Elvis," Mark observed, directing his remark to a waitress who stood with the Chandlers, smiling at the commotion the old lady was causing.

When they finally sat down and their order was taken, Dorry said, "Mae Mae, you are a celebrity!"

"No, baby," she chuckled. "Mae Mae just old! The older Mae Mae git, the crazier these people act! I do love 'em though."

"You two keep talking," Mark interjected as he slid out of the booth. "I need to speak with someone about a fax machine to send this drawing of the food stone to Dylan. Hopefully, it will be okay with them for us to hang out here and wait for Dylan's call back. He has my cell."

Watching him go, Mae Mae said, "You got a sweet man. He's like my Jerold."

"Yes, ma'am," Dorry said. "Mark is a wonderful husband. And a wonderful father." Changing the subject, she asked, "Mae Mae, Dr. Carver left the food stone to you. Did he not have any children?"

"No," she replied. "He never got married. Too caught up in his work. He wrote me one time 'bout how he was sweet on a lady teacher in Tuskegee, but I'm thinkin' she got tired of waitin' on the man! That was durin' the same time them big Eastern newspapers was after him. They said he wadn' a scientist 'cause he gave the credit to the Lord.

They asked him how he made his discoveries and he told 'em how he'd get up every mornin' in the dark. He said that God drawed back the curtain on what he was 'posed to do. An' them newspapers ate 'im up fer it! Said a scientist got to have a better method than that! Look to me like that method worked out pretty good!"

Mae Mae huffed. "All them criticizers . . . anybody build a statue of them? They in history books? The vice president of the United States of America come to *their* funerals?" Dorry was shaking her head. "I didn' think so!" Mae Mae sat back with an audible, "Hmmph," as if she were through, but began talking again almost immediately.

"The only thing Uncle Gee said on the subject was when he told 'em, 'Be careful now,' he said. 'Just 'cause you don't understand something—or even believe it—that don't mean it ain't true!'" She suddenly laughed. "He was always smilin' and happy. An' he was always *doin'*! Didn' never slow down. I learned that from him. I don't slow down. I see all these people sixty, seventy years old . . . young people! They actin' all creaky and sad. Not Mae Mae!

"Uncle Gee—ever' letter he wrote me—he talked about bein' a example. And that's what Mae Mae still tries to be! 'Cause people are watchin' and learnin'—specially the chirren—and they gon' do what you do! Every day I think, *What kinda world would this world be . . . if ever'body in it acted just like me?*"

"Say that again, Mae Mae," Dorry said and wrote it on the front of her notepad as the old lady repeated the words slowly.

Just then, Mark reappeared as the waitress put the food on the table. "Got him," Mark declared as he held up the cell phone. "Fax is away. As soon as they get it, Abby's gonna look at it and they'll call us back."

As they ate, Dorry and Mark continued to pepper Mae Mae with questions about her famous uncle. Both were fascinated that the object belonged to a person who had accomplished so much and that the relic itself seemed to somehow be a part of that achievement.

After finishing their meal, the three drank coffee and talked until, at last, the cell phone chirped. Raising his eyebrows, Mark said, "Here we go!" He opened the phone. "Mark Chandler."

Mae Mae whispered to Dorry, "He answers the phone like the police, don't he?" Dorry stifled a laugh, but was intent on the one-sided conversation she was hearing.

"Okay with me," Mark said. "So it was clear enough? . . . Yeah, we're here with Mae Mae right now . . ." Mark laughed. "That's right, we call her Mae Mae . . . Sure. Fine as far as I'm concerned. Do I need a pen?" Dorry began scrambling in her purse, but Mark held up his hand. "Okay," he said. "Tell me."

Dorry and Mae Mae watched Mark closely as he listened. They saw his mouth drop open. "No way," he said.

"What? What?!" Dorry demanded. "What does it say?!"

Mark, listening closely to Dylan, but looking Dorry in the eye, put his finger forcefully to his lips and turned away from her in the booth. "Dylan, say that again." He paused. "You don't have any idea how unbelievable that is. When do you get home?" Another pause. "Okay. Us too. We have a midmorning flight out of Memphis tomorrow. Can you and Abby just plan on being at our house tomorrow night? . . . Yeah . . . Yeah, I think she needs to be in on it . . . It would take too long to explain and I'm not sure I understand anyway. Listen, is nine o'clock too late? That'll give us some time with Michael and we can have him in bed

by the time you two get there . . . If you don't mind . . .
Good! Okay, see you then . . . you too. Bye-bye."

As Mark slowly turned around to face Dorry and Mae
Mae again, he closed the phone and placed it on the table.
Dorry couldn't tell if her husband was stunned or bewil-
dered . . . or both. "I'm assuming Abby translated it?" she
asked finally.

He didn't move a muscle, but said, "Uh-huh."

Dorry glanced at Mae Mae, who seemed somewhat
amused. Then, taking a deep breath to calm herself, she
asked, "Mark? What does the script on the food stone say?"

As if a trance were broken, Mark looked first at Dorry,
then Mae Mae, and leaned forward. Quietly he said, "Abby
said it translates to—are you ready for this?—*By your hand,
the people shall be fed.*"

Mae Mae popped her dentures back and forth as, for a
long moment, the three stared at each other in astonishment. "Well," she finally said in her soft drawl, "I tol' you it
was a food stone."

Once the initial shock wore off, Mae Mae dug the food
stone out of her handbag and laid it on the table in front of
her, fanning the leather cord out in a circle. "I brought it wif
us," she said simply. Touching the object's surface with her
fingers, Mae Mae said to Mark, "Say them words again."

"By your hand," Mark said slowly, "the people shall be
fed."

Mae Mae picked up the object and held it close to her
face, staring intently as if to somehow see into it. "The
people shall be fed," she murmured. "Lord, Lord. How
many people did Uncle Gee feed wearin' this?"

"How many people is he still feeding?" Dorry asked.
"Think about that!"

"Mae Mae?" Mark began. "When we were at your house, you said that your grandfather wore this and that it was known as a food stone long before George Washington Carver became . . . well, George Washington Carver . . . know what I mean?" She nodded. "Anyway," he continued, "do you have any idea who might have had it before your grandfather?"

"No," Mae Mae answered.

"What are you thinking?" Dorry asked.

"I don't know, really," Mark replied. "I am barely getting my brain around this." He shook his head in quick little jerks. "I mean, this thing came from Africa . . . right?" He threw a questioning glance in Mae Mae's direction. She nodded. "In Africa, it was already known as a food stone . . . though we can make the assumption that the translation had been lost or forgotten years ago. So somehow, this piece acquired a reputation of having something to do with producing food or feeding the hungry . . . and this reputation was perpetuated by people who did not know what the writing said! That makes no sense."

Mae Mae broke into a full-fledged grin. "You thinkin' maybe it's magic, aintcha?"

"No," Dorry said. "Of course not." She paused. "I don't think. I mean, that's ridiculous, right?"

"Let me say it like this, baby," Mae Mae said. "They may or may not be magic in this here food stone. But Mae Mae knows for sure . . . there *is* magic inside you."

"I don't—," Dorry started to say.

"What Mae Mae's sayin' is, they may be all kind of magic in this here rock, but you set there waitin' for the magic to happen and *do nothin'*? Tha's exactly what you gonna get. Nothin'! On the other hand, you choose to do somethin' special? You gon' get somethin' special." Having made her point, the old woman sat back, crossed her arms, and said, "There ya go. Tha's it."

Pausing in their conversation as the waitress poured fresh cups of coffee, they were aware that the restaurant had almost emptied its lunch crowd, but no one seemed to mind their continued presence. As the waitress walked away, Dorry said something to Mae Mae that had been on her mind. "Earlier today, you called the food stone 'an inspiration' for your uncle. Is that all it was?"

Mae Mae thought for a bit, then spoke. "I'm sure it meant a lot to him 'cause it was from his daddy, but mostly it was a reminder of the choice."

Mark and Dorry looked puzzled, as if they'd missed something. "I don't understand," Mark said.

"Let's put it this way. You think my Uncle George Washington Carver made a difference in this world?"

"Of course. Absolutely," they answered.

"You'd be right. Now, let me ask you this. Do you think they's some people that never make a difference in this world?"

Mark and Dorry hesitated, then answered yes, that they believed that to be true.

"And tha's where you'd be dead wrong!" Mae Mae said as she pointed her finger. "Everybody—every single body—makes a difference! But there is a *choice* that determines what kinda difference you will make. Most folks don't see how important they are . . . how much they matter to all of us. So they never choose to do somethin' special wif their lives. And *not* makin' a choice? That *is* a choice . . . a lost one."

"Wow." Mark opened his eyes widely and looked at Dorry. "I never thought of it that way, but it's true."

Dorry opened her purse and, after rummaging through it, removed the first relic and placed it on the table beside the food stone. Except for the food stone's leather cord and slight variation in shape, the two were almost identical. The major difference, they already knew, was in the inscription. "By your hand, the people shall live," Dorry said and looked up. "Mae Mae, was there a choice involved with this one, do you think?"

"Yes, baby, I do. An' I think they was just as many choices wrapped up in that one as this one." The old woman picked up the food stone by its cord and, holding it aloft, said, "The difference here is that we know some of the history. An' we know that Uncle Gee understood about the danger of a *lost* choice. Tha's why he pushed folks to make one."

"What do you mean?" asked Mark.

"Uncle Gee would put this stone on a person and ask 'em, 'Do you pledge to do somethin' special with your life?' He'd make 'em answer. I know he done it lots of times 'cause Dr. Patterson—that's the man was president at Tuskegee when Uncle Gee passed—he wrote me a letter and told me so. He said Uncle Gee put this 'round his neck many a time and asked him that very question. He told me that wadn' a day go by that he didn' strive to live up to the choice he made."

She held the food stone higher, studied it as it turned on the cord, then put it back on the table. "Come 'round here, son," she said to Mark.

"Ma'am?" he asked, not certain what she wanted him to do.

"Come 'roun' here to me and get down where I can see you." Mark eased out of the booth and stepped to the old woman's side. "Kneel down here," she said and he did.

"I want to give this food stone to you."

"Oh, Mae Mae," Dorry gasped, bringing her hand to her mouth. "Are you sure? It belongs in your family."

"Now then," she said, "in one way Mae Mae ain' got no more family. An' in one way, we *all* family. Ever'body in the world. We sho' enough touchin' each other's lives, ain't we?"

"Yes, ma'am," Dorry said.

"Anyhow, Mae Mae's almost a thousand years old, and I want you, Mark, to have this. It'll be a gift for you to one day give that son of yours. Lean your head down here."

As Mark lowered his head, the tiny old black woman reached up and placed the leather cord around his neck. She then cradled his face in her hands and said, "Mark, do you pledge to do something special wif your life?"

Mark reached up and covered her left hand that lay cool against his cheek with his right hand. "Yes, ma'am. I promise."

She took the first relic in her other hand and reached across to Dorry. Mae Mae placed it in Dorry's palm, but kept her hand there, interlocking fingers with the younger woman, holding the object between them. "Baby girl," she said to Dorry, who now had tears in her eyes, "do you pledge to do something special wif *your* life?"

"Yes," Dorry said. "I do."

"All right then," she said as she popped her dentures. "I'm gon' expect it. Now take Mae Mae home. I love you, but I'm wore out."

❧ NINE

IT WAS TEN MINUTES UNTIL NINE O'CLOCK.
Knowing that Dylan would be on time, Dorry was making a last-minute run through the house to be certain that everything was clean and in order. She had never met Abby and wanted to create a good first impression.

Their flight from Memphis had gotten in just before noon. Retrieving Michael, they had taken the time to eat lunch with Dorry's parents and still were at home by two-thirty. It was a perfect fall afternoon, and Mark and Dorry had spent most of it outdoors playing with their son. Around six, Mark and Michael had cooked dinner while Dorry caught up on the e-mail deluge from work. She was, at least, relieved to see that there was nothing due by tomorrow morning.

Now Michael was in bed—already asleep—and Mark made a fresh pot of coffee as Dorry removed a Matchbox dump truck from between the cushions of the living room couch. "How many of these things does Michael have?"

she asked as she walked to the kitchen and rolled the toy across the counter to her husband.

Mark deftly caught the truck when it fell from the edge and put it on top of the refrigerator. "I don't know," he said. "But I'll tell you how many he's gonna have if I step on another one with my bare feet in the middle of the night. I stepped on that little tank in the bathroom last week and almost killed myself!"

The doorbell rang. "There they are," Dorry said. "You let them in and I'll be right back. I want to check on Michael before we get started."

Twenty-seven-year-old Abby Warner was tall and tanned. Her shoulder-length, light-brown hair was tied back into a ponytail. Blond highlights, combined with her clear, blue eyes, framed her effortless smile.

"Hi! Come on in," Mark said as Abby, then Dylan, entered through the front door. Dorry arrived on the scene seconds later and hugged Dylan as she and Mark were introduced to the archaeologist who had become his girlfriend.

Moving the group into the living room, Dorry said, "Dylan, she's beautiful!"

"Really? Do you think so?" Dylan responded, kidding. "I hadn't even noticed *that* about her." Mark and Dorry laughed as Abby rolled her eyes and blushed.

"Okay," Dorry said, "let's leave her alone until we get to know her—*then* we can tease her unmercifully." Everyone laughed. "Abby, you come with me. We'll get our coffee the way we like it and these two can just take what we bring them." As the guys made themselves comfortable on the couch, Dorry and Abby disappeared into the kitchen. Mark winked at Dylan. They had both sensed that, for some reason, Dorry had instantly taken a liking to the younger woman.

In the kitchen, the two women did indeed bond immediately. Dorry showed Abby the pictures of Michael on the refrigerator and asked about Abby's childhood. She was very interested in Abby's choice of Dartmouth for college and learned that it was one of the only schools in the United States offering a degree in classical archaeology. When the coffee was ready, there had never been a lull in the conversation.

"Here we go," Dorry said, lifting the tray of cups, cream, and sugar. Abby followed her into the living room where Dylan and Mark were already hovered over the coffee table. Dylan was examining the food stone with a magnifying glass.

"Make room, guys," Dorry said as they quickly cleared the table. "You haven't started talking without us, have you?"

"No, just looking," Dylan said, "but holy moly, this is really unbelievable."

"Holy moly?" Dorry asked. Mark grinned. He could see that his wife was deciding whether or not to torment Dylan about his choice of words.

Sensing a challenge to the term, however, Dylan spoke first. "Holy moly is perfectly acceptable," he said with an air of mock superiority. "In the dictionary, the expression is listed under *M* for 'moly, holy.' Its definition? 'Holy moly— a degree of holiness somewhere between mackerel and cow.' Look it up."

"Okay, okay," Mark laughed as Dorry and Abby rolled their eyes. "Let's get to it. Dylan, tell us what you think is so unbelievable about this."

Dylan slid off the couch and, on his knees at the coffee table, looked through his magnifying glass at the food stone again.

"Well, the similarities for one thing," he said, "but those are obvious. Abby, you're the expert—I'm out of my league here."

The pony-tailed archaeologist crowded in closely. "Let me see."

Dylan shifted to allow her room while Mark moved the tray with the sugar and cream to the dining room. He then transferred the lamp at the end of the couch directly to the coffee table. "That better?" he asked, and when they answered in the affirmative, Mark joined everyone else on the living room floor.

"I'm surprised the scripting is so clearly maintained," Abby said. "There is wear, obviously, some fading, but these are beautiful pieces."

Dorry, looking over Abby's shoulder, asked, "Why are you surprised about the scripting?"

Without taking her eyes from the two objects, Abby answered, "I am assuming these are the same relative age— if not exactly the same age—because of size, color, degree of declension, and certainly because of the similar translations. But . . . in a relic this old, one would expect much more wear around the edges of the script cuts." She held the objects up into the light for everyone to see. "Notice how sharply defined the carving is? If one were to view each separate indentation as a tiny canyon, the rim of the cliff is a sudden drop. It is not a smoothed or rounded edge as one might expect after centuries of exposure to the elements."

Abby used the magnifying glass again. "I want to look at these under a scope, if you don't mind my taking them to the museum's lab"—she paused—"but what I see here . . ." She looked up and thought for a moment. Placing the pieces carefully back onto the coffee table, Abby continued in a matter-of-fact tone. "Two specifics catch my attention. One is the condition of the items—which is what we've been talking about. I know this one was found in or around water, correct?"

"Yes, correct," the Chandlers confirmed.

"Just a cursory examination will tell you that this thing has not spent much of its life *outdoors*, forget 'in the water.' And both objects are the same in that regard. They are simply not eroded sufficiently to have been anything but . . ." Abby frowned.

"Anything but what?" Dorry asked.

"Personally protected." Dylan finished the sentence for her. Turning to Abby, who still seemed deep in thought, he said, "That's what has you thrown, isn't it? You think they've both been personally protected—passed down like an heirloom—for two thousand or so years?"

Abby sighed. "But that's absurd . . . right?"

"Weeeell," Dylan drew out the word. "I think it's stretching the realm a bit. I don't know, Ab . . . to think an object might be intentionally transferred from person to person for two millennia? As empires are rising and falling? I mean, that's longer than civilizations have lasted in that part of the world."

"Logically, I agree," Abby allowed. "And archaeologically, it doesn't make sense . . . but *look* at them." She placed the objects in Dylan's hands somewhat defiantly. "You have to admit . . . you've seen Apache artifacts less than two hundred years old in worse shape than these. I don't think this piece"—she indicated the one Michael found—"has been exposed to the elements for even a hundred years, much less two thousand. And this one . . ." Abby picked up the food stone by its leather cord. "This one is in better shape than the other! The only possibility I can imagine is that they have been protected in some way since they were cast."

Dylan nodded. "It's strange, but I don't disagree with anything you've said."

"And like *you* said, Dylan," Mark interjected, "she's the expert."

"Yeah, she is," Dylan concurred.

"Abby," Dorry broke in. "A minute ago, you said that there were two things—specifics, you called them—two specifics that caught your attention. One was the condition of these pieces. What was the other?"

"Location," Abby said simply. "Both pieces were collected on the North American continent. Not unusual really, but telling, just the same."

"How so?"

Abby shrugged. "Think of it this way. This continent is an archaeological net. The world's objects of scarcity and value have always gravitated to financially superior and culturally free societies . . . and that's what we have in North America. Mathematically, give Earth another twenty thousand years, and everything will end up here."

"So this one," Mark said, "the food stone, came from Africa in the mid-1800s. And this one, Michael's, was—"

"—was not in that creek for long," Abby interrupted. "In an archaeological sense anyway."

Conscious of the need to take a break, Dorry said, "Mark, you three go into the kitchen and make some fresh coffee. Tell Abby and Dylan the whole story about Mae Mae and George Washington Carver. I'm gonna check on Michael and do a couple of quick searches on the Internet. There's pie in the fridge."

Twenty minutes later, Dorry eased back into the kitchen

and joined the others who were seated around the breakfast table. Mark was almost through with the story—telling
Dylan and Abby about George Washington Carver's funeral
and how Mae Mae had gotten the food stone. As he talked,
Abby held the food stone in her hand.

"I don't want to sound weird or anything," Mark said as
he finished, "but I swear, something happened to me when
she put that thing around my neck and I promised to do
something with my life."

"Something *special* with your life," Dorry corrected.

"Right. Something special."

"Something happened to you . . . in what way?" Abby
asked.

"Honestly, I'm not even sure how to explain what I felt,"
Mark said. He lifted his hands, then let them fall in a futile
gesture. "In a way, I suppose I have always intended to do
something special with my life, but when I said it—or as
Mae Mae said, when I 'made it a choice'—I felt a sense of
power, or purpose . . . or certainty . . . assurance . . . something."

"I'm not even getting this," Dylan said. He held out his
hand to Abby, silently requesting the food stone. As he took
it, he shook his head as if to clear it, then spoke slowly.
"Okay. This thing translates out to . . ." He looked expectantly at Abby.

She said, "By your hand, the people shall be fed."

Dylan looked at the other three and repeated Abby's
words. "By your hand, the people shall be fed." He paused
dramatically. "Fed . . . fed? And George Washington Carver
was wearing this? George Washington Carver? I mean,
guys, the odds against any human being achieving what he
did . . . and then you tell me he was wearing this? I barely
believe it."

"Excuse me," Dorry said as she raised her hand. "Let me rattle our collective cage a bit more." She fanned out a stack of paper. "Fresh from my printer . . . plumbed from the depths of cyberspace." Turning to her husband, she asked, "Mark, did you tell Abby and Dylan about Patterson?"

"Patterson?" Mark appeared lost. "I'm not sure *I* remember. Tell me who he was again."

Dorry shuffled the pages she'd brought to the table. "Lucky for us . . . I take notes," she said to Abby as she waggled her eyebrows up and down. "Dr. Frederick Patterson was the president of Tuskegee Institute when Carver died. Mae Mae met him at the funeral in 1943."

"Yeah, I remember now."

"Do you remember that Mae Mae said Dr. Patterson wrote a letter to her? In it, he told her that Carver put the food stone around his neck several times and asked him to pledge to do something special with his life. You remember this, right?"

"Yeah, I do," Mark replied. "He told her that he tried to live up to that choice he made every day."

"Well . . . he made good on his promise," Dorry said. "You wouldn't believe the Internet search hits when I typed in his name. Listen to this." She read a sentence she had highlighted on one of the pages from the printer. "As founder of the United Negro College Fund, Dr. Frederick Patterson richly deserved the Presidential Medal of Freedom bestowed upon him personally by President Reagan. Dr. Patterson, the first African-American member of the American Red Cross Central Committee, created research institutes, schools, public grants . . ." Dorry looked up. "It would take a week to read everything this guy did. It's incredible."

Dylan was leaning over the table with his mouth open while Dorry read. When she finished, he held up the food stone and asked, "And that guy . . . Patterson? That guy had this around his neck?"

"Several times, evidently," Dorry replied as the others gawked at her. "Hang on. Wait till you hear this!" Then, to Mark she said, "Did you tell them about Henry Wallace?"

Mark nodded.

"The vice president?" Abby asked.

"Um-hmm," Dorry confirmed. "There are about ten times the number of Internet hits on him. Now, you know that he wandered the woods with Carver when he was a child in Iowa."

"Wait a minute," Dylan said incredulously. "I wasn't connecting these dots before. Carver put the food stone on this kid in Iowa?"

Dorry nodded, and Dylan looked at Mark. "This is who you were telling us a few minutes ago who . . . *this* kid grew up to be the secretary of agriculture and vice president of the United States?!!" Dylan was about to come across the table.

"Well, here," Dorry said. "Let me just send everybody over the edge." She flipped some papers. "Okay . . . secretary of agriculture in '33 . . . vice president in 1940. That was under Roosevelt, by the way . . . hang on . . . here we go. Henry Wallace developed some of the first hybrid corn varieties, and by planting his hybrid seed, U.S. farmers doubled and tripled their per-acre yield."

Dorry glanced up. Mark's eyes were wide as he slowly shook his head. "Oh, just wait," she said turning pages as she searched for a specific, highlighted piece. "This next bit is . . . well, here it is. Okay," she said to the others, "this is from just *one* of the Web sites with this info . . . you ready?"

"Go. Shoot," they said.

Dorry read, "'In 1940, shortly after being elected vice president, Wallace traveled to Mexico and was appalled at the corn production in a country where corn was the most important part of a Mexican family's diet. Their per-acre yield was drastically lower than that of American farmers who planted hybrid varieties. The vice president soon created an agricultural station in Mexico to develop corn varieties adapted for the climate and soil of that region.'"

Dorry looked up and said, "Still reading—follow me here." She continued. "'One of the first scientists to join the station started by Wallace was a man named Norman Borlaug. Twenty years after the station was built, corn production in Mexico had doubled and wheat production had increased fivefold. Borlaug won the Nobel Peace Prize in 1970 because of the work he did at the station.'" Dorry lifted her head.

No one spoke. They simply stared at her as she held the papers printed from the Internet out in front of her. "So why did Borlaug get the Nobel Prize? It says here—get this—that the work at that station in Mexico in expanding yields of corn, wheat, and rice prevented worldwide famine . . . and over the years, the lives of a billion people were saved."

"A billion?" Abby whispered.

"Yeah, billion," Dorry answered. "With a *b.*"

"Uh-huh," Dylan restated, "with a *b. B* for billion and *b* for butterfly. This, my friends, is a textbook illustration of the butterfly effect."

"The what?" Mark asked.

"The butterfly effect—sensitive dependence upon initial conditions."

"In English, please," Abby prodded.

Ignoring her, Dylan continued. "In 1963, Edward Lorenz presented a paper to the New York Academy of Sciences that created an uproar because of its straightforward and unembellished accuracy. He called it the butterfly effect. Simply stated, the butterfly effect says that a butterfly can flap its wings on one side of the world and set molecules of air in motion . . . that in turn set other molecules of air in motion . . . which set *other* molecules of air in motion— that can eventually create a hurricane on the other side of the world." Dylan spread his hands apart like an entertainer receiving applause and repeated, "The butterfly effect."

As they digested this new thought, the four friends each quietly reacted in a different way. Dylan, the last to speak, remained perfectly still, simply staring at the others. Abby slowly twirled the end of her ponytail around the forefinger of her right hand. Mark ran his thumbnail back and forth in the groove of the table's edge while Dorry absentmindedly sipped her coffee, which was cold.

Mark broke the silence first. "So in human terms, you're saying that Carver is an example of the butterfly effect."

"Without a doubt," Dylan said. "Look at it this way: Carver influenced Wallace, who set up the station in Mexico. The station in Mexico produced Borlaug . . . who directed its efforts. And the final result was that worldwide famine was averted and a billion lives saved."

"Actually," Abby interjected, "that wasn't the final result. That *particular* storm put in motion by the butterfly will never die. It's still gathering strength. Think of the things yet to be accomplished—the lives that are sure to be touched—

by those billion people who wouldn't even be alive if . . ."
Her voice trailed off as she raised her eyebrows in wonder.

Mark finished the sentence. "Who wouldn't even be
alive if Carver hadn't taken time with that little boy . . ."

"Who grew up to be vice president . . . ," Dylan said.

"And started the station in Mexico . . . ," Abby added as
they watched each other wide-eyed.

"Holy moly!" Dorry exclaimed as they burst out laughing.

Mark stood and leaned against the wall, still adrift in the
concept of one life having so much meaning. "Wrap your
brain around this," he said. "These billion people. They are
a part of only *one* move Carver made. All the peanut stuff?
That was a totally different flap of his wings—to stick with
the same metaphor. Consider that! You think the 'little boy'
connection is big? When Carver flapped his wings and created the uses for the peanut, how many billions have been
affected by that?"

"Here's my question," Dylan said standing up. He moved
the food stone to the center of the table. "Where has this
thing been?" He looked sharply at each of the others. "By
your hand, the people shall be fed?" Then, Dylan moved
Michael's object to the center of the table. "And this! By
your hand, the people shall *live*? What does *that* mean? And
where has *this* one been?"

Dylan turned to his girlfriend. "Ab, think about it," he
said. "You feel that the condition of these objects indicates
personal handling. Okay, I agree. Now . . . I want to know
who handled them."

❧ TEN

MARK HAD RESCUED DORRY FROM A ROUGH morning at the *Post* in time to join Dylan and Abby for lunch at a diner downtown. It was their fifth time together since their first meeting as a foursome. They were discovering quickly how much they enjoyed each other's company and to a person were increasingly interested in the broadening mystery of the relics.

Mark's experience as a detective had made him the acknowledged leader of their quest, and at his direction, they had each agreed to shoulder separate tasks—exploring different angles—for information. Mark sent requests to the data banks of the FBI, Scotland Yard, and Interpol hoping a "stolen items report" might include a description of one of the objects. Unlike news releases, which report broadly, he explained, arrest reports required itemized listings. Still, he was not optimistic.

Dorry worked a reporter's angle with friends in the research department at the *Post*. Focusing on archaeological finds, she narrowed the search to "leaded bronze pieces weighing less than 200 grams" and waded through mountains of articles—most of them pre-Internet from AP or UPI.

As they ordered and ate sandwiches, the four friends tried to lay out their facts and questions in as orderly a fashion as possible. As Abby listed her findings, mentioning again that the two relics were hollow, Dylan stopped her. "Hey, here's a question," he said. "Are both hollow in the same way?"

Noting Abby's furrowed brow, he explained, "I mean . . . were they cast in hollow form? Or were they left hollowed by pressure—like when you bend a car antenna until it breaks. If you do that to an antenna in two places, you are left with a piece that is closed at the ends and hollow in the middle."

"I see where you are going with this," Abby said as she narrowed her eyes to concentrate. "If I ran a scope on the objects and concluded pressure closure . . ." She paused.

"What?" Dorry asked.

"Pressure closure would prove the objects are in secondary—broken—form."

"And that would mean . . . ?" Dorry prodded.

"It would mean that we have a new question," Abby said. "And that would be: What did these objects look like in their primary form?" She sat back in her chair and crossed her arms. "I made the assumption that the relics were relatively unchanged because of the lack of erosion on their surface. But that doesn't preclude the possibility of a catastrophic event. And in archaeological terms, that can be anything from a meteor strike to a hammer blow. It's the opposite of erosion, which happens over time."

Abby was quiet for a bit, thinking, then breathed deeply.

"This gives me a direction, at least," she said and turned to Dylan. "Tell Mark and Dorry about Perasi."

"Well," Dylan began, "at the museum, we have this one guy, Perasi—that's his first name; he's Indian—he is a computer god! Short, stubby kid. He never goes home . . . I swear he sleeps there. He's with Library and Archives. Anyway," Dylan said with a sly expression, "I bring him pizza every now and then, so he's my buddy, you know? Well, two or three months ago, he got his new computer platform up and rocking . . . cutting-edge software. I'm telling you, this is a state-of-the-art, monster system. We're only one of four museums in the U.S. that even has one of these. Perasi says there are governments of countries that don't have systems this powerful! I'm telling you, he can do anything. This kid could create a program to determine how many inches of string are used in the basketball nets owned by the Boy's Clubs of America east of the Mississippi River!

"So for me . . . us . . . Perasi has created a massive search engine designed specifically to search photographs, paintings, statuary, videotape, microfiche . . . that kind of thing. He fed 3-D representations of the two objects into the program and the computer will sweep for items of the same likeness that appear in any visual medium."

Dorry was amazed. "Is that possible?" she asked.

"Absolutely," he said excitedly. "I was only asking him to go through *our* museum archives and he said, 'How about the world?' And the kid was not joking! Just to show me what could be done, while I was standing there, he ran a program that searched for 'United States presidents shooting a bow and arrow.' He designated 'color photos only' to narrow the field and in seventeen minutes showed me one of Eisenhower and one of Nixon!"

"So exactly what will he search," Mark asked, "and when does he start?"

"Perasi is programming as we speak. He says he'll be ready to fire it up tonight. We aren't on a deadline, so I told him to sweep everything he can. He is programming for photographs—published and nonpublished—which means the computer will also search museum collections and news archives around the world. He's scanning paintings, carvings, and statuary *and* cross-referencing all of it . . . in case there's a painting of a statue or a photograph of a carving."

"Great job, guys," Mark said as they noticed the time and stood up from the table. "Let's keep plugging away."

LEAVING THE DINER, EVERYONE HAD AGREED TO meet again at four o'clock Saturday afternoon. It had been Tuesday, and five days, they felt, would have allowed time to work on their respective projects and, hopefully, have some progress to report. However, Thursday evening the telephone at the Chandlers' house rang. Dylan was on the other end of the line, muttering, "Come on! Come on!"

"Hello," Dorry answered. It was eight-thirty. She had just put Michael to bed and was about to take a bath.

"Dorry! Is Mark there? Can you get him on the other phone? I need to talk to both of you."

Less than twenty seconds later, Mark picked up. "Hey, Dylan. What's going on?"

"Are you both there?"

"Yeah, we're here," the Chandlers responded.

"We have to meet in the morning," Dylan said in a rush. "Before work. Unless we could do it tonight. But you have

Michael. I can't find Abby anyway. We have to get together in the morning. If we—"

"Dylan! Hey, whoa! Stop!" Mark said. "Take a breath. What in the heck is going on?"

"I'm not kidding," Dylan said. "I'm at the museum with Perasi. He called me and said to come down. Abby's at a movie with her lab assistant, and I guess her cell phone's off. I'm here and we have a hit on this program. I made a call and, man! This changes everything. Oh, man! Can we meet in the morning?"

Mark was on a cordless phone and had made his way to the bedroom where Dorry had originally answered Dylan's call. They listened to him babble excitedly as they watched each other. Mark furrowed his brow and made an expression on his face to his wife that asked, *What's up with this?* Dorry shrugged an *I have no idea* as Mark spoke again. "Dylan. Slow down, brother. Tell me what you have."

"No," Dylan answered. "Not yet. I have one more call to make; let me get to Ab—then we might *really* have something to talk about."

"Dylan!" Dorry said. "You have to—"

"Just trust me on this. Where can we meet in the morning and how early?"

"Well—," Mark started.

"How about the coffee shop right across from the museum?" Dylan pushed. "I'm gonna spend the night here."

"Seriously?" Dorry asked, raising her eyebrows at Mark, who still stood in the bedroom with the cordless phone.

"Yeah, absolutely. I have to get to Abby, but other than that, I'm watching this computer all night. Can we say six o'clock?"

"Whew!" Mark tossed a questioning glance at Dorry,

who quickly calculated the timing of taking care of her child, then nodded. "Yeah," he answered, "six will be fine."

"Okay, don't be late. See you there," Dylan said and hung up before the Chandlers could say good-bye.

The next morning, Abby and Dylan were waiting out-side the tiny restaurant when Mark and Dorry walked up the sidewalk at five minutes until six. Due to the early hour, the Chandlers had been able to park on the street just down from the coffee shop. As they greeted the younger couple, Dylan opened the door and said, "Hi, guys. Come on!"

Abby hugged Dorry and said secretively, "Oh, gosh! I'd blurt everything out right now, but he'd kill me. We spent the night here . . . in the museum, I mean. I am sooo excited!"

"*You* spent the night here too?" Dorry said as they took their jackets off and sat down at the farthest table from the door. Thanks to Dylan, there were already cups and an insulated pot of coffee on the table, which Dorry began pouring immediately.

"Yes," Abby said, now speaking to all of them. "I went to a movie last night with some friends, and when I got home, Dylan was in the parking lot of my apartment complex. I had forgotten to turn my phone back on when I left the theater. Once he showed me what you're about to see . . . well, I went back to the museum and stayed. Perasi is still there."

"*What* then?" Mark said. "Don't keep us in suspense any longer. What?"

Dylan laid a manila envelope on the table, opened it, and reached inside. "Breathe deeply, children," he said mysteri-ously and pulled a sheet of paper from the envelope. "What you are about to see will amaze and astound you."

"Didn't I see you doing your magic act on a cruise ship?" Mark asked with feigned sincerity.

"Hush," Dorry commanded. "Go, Dylan."

Before he set the paper on the table, however, Dylan placed his hand over a part of it. When the page was displayed before them, Mark and Dorry saw that it was a computer printout, in color, of a painting. The painting, set in a gold gilded frame, was that of a warrior. Dylan's hand covered a portion of the warrior's image. "This painting belongs to a museum in Venice, Italy, and is part of a collection that once belonged to Charles VII of France." He looked down at the paper under his hand and whispered, "Do you know who this is?"

Dorry stared intently. The figure in the painting wore white armor and stood in front of an army. Dylan's palm hid the warrior's face and arms. As he slowly slid his hand to the top of the painting, the face of the armored figure was revealed first. Dorry saw that it was the face of a young girl and said cautiously, "Joan of Arc?"

With those words, Dylan removed his hand from the rest of the painting. Dorry's fingers flew to her mouth as she gasped. "I don't believe it," she said. "Mark, do you see?" He nodded.

Both arms of the figure were held above her head. In her left hand, she held a sword. But in her right, the Maid of Orleans, Joan of Arc, the seventeen-year-old girl who led her king's army to victory, held one of the relics. It was clasped tightly in her palm, but the image was unmistakable.

"The museum's director told me that the painting's subject is, supposedly, the Battle for Orleans in 1429," Dylan said. "I looked it up. She won."

"I don't even know what to say," Mark exclaimed.

"Don't say anything yet," Abby said. "Just wait."

"There's more?" Dorry said, looking quickly at Abby, then Dylan, and back to the painting of Joan.

"Yes, there is," Dylan said as he reached into the envelope again. "Check this out." He pushed a printed photograph across to Mark. Dorry shifted to get a good angle in order to view the picture. It was of four men. One was seated behind a desk, the others posing behind him. Plainly visible in the photograph, closer to the camera, in fact, than the men, was the object of the computer's search. It was sitting on top of the desk.

"Who . . . ?" Mark murmured as he carefully touched the relic in the picture with his finger.

"Oskar Schindler," Abby said. "*Schindler's List*? Did you ever see the Spielberg movie?" Dorry nodded blankly. "That's the real guy. He's the one sitting at the desk." To Dylan, she said, "Show them the rest."

Dylan removed a stack of prints from the envelope and began laying them one by one in front of Mark and Dorry. Schindler signing papers. Schindler with a uniformed Nazi. Schindler laughing. Eating. With a woman on his lap. Eight photographs in all. Every picture had the desk in it, and the object was featured prominently on the desk in every shot. Dylan lay one more down, a ninth picture. It was a candid photo of Oskar Schindler—with the relic in his hand.

Mark and Dorry were dumbfounded. They couldn't take their eyes off the evidence in front of them—evidence that the objects truly *were* valued for some reason and passed from person to person throughout the years.

"Incidentally," Dylan said as he sat with his arms crossed, waiting patiently for the Chandlers to come up for air, "a Web search registers 491,000 hits on Joan of Arc, and Perasi's computer scanned 58,641 images of her in order to uncover the painting in Italy. Schindler was easier—27,900 hits and these nine shots showed up among 2,556 searched images."

"Wow," Mark said.

"Tell them, Dylan," Abby prodded.

"Tell us what?" Dorry demanded.

"There's more," Dylan said. "We've only been running for two days, but the program has captured a big fish."

"Bigger than this?" Mark said, indicating the papers scattered over the tabletop.

"I think so," Dylan replied as he slid the manila envelope across the table, never losing eye contact with Mark. "You will too. Open it."

Hesitating only for a second, Mark lifted the flap of the envelope. Removing the one remaining sheet of paper, he saw that it was another printout of a color photograph—two photographs actually—printed side by side on the one page. The picture was a close-up front and back view of one of the relics. In the bottom right corner of each photo was the designation "Item 267—lot-4932881.pe.L/nfd."

Mark frowned. "The computer found . . . just a photograph of it?" he said. "By itself?"

Dorry was initially confused, as well. Then, grabbing the page from her husband, she quickly examined it, looked up at Abby, and back at the photo.

"Do you see?" Abby asked urgently.

"I do," Dorry answered. "What do we do now?"

"What?" Mark said. "What do you see?"

"Mark," Dorry said, never shifting her gaze from the pictures. "This is not one of ours. This is another one."

Mark drew back and looked at Dylan. "Really?" he asked. "This is a totally different object?"

"Yes, it is. See the edges," Dylan said, pointing. "The script, at first glance, all kind of looks the same to me, but I knew it was a new object—new to us anyway—by the edges. Abby confirmed that the message is different too. Good pic. Very nice resolution. She was able to do the translation with the photograph."

Mark and Dorry swung their heads swiftly to Abby. "What does it say?" Dorry asked.

"By your hand," Abby said quietly, "the people shall be free."

"Free." Mark closed his eyes. "Live. Fed." He paused. "And now 'free.'" Opening his eyes, he asked Dylan, "Where is *this* one?"

"You'll love this," Dylan said. "It's in the Smithsonian . . . in D.C. I couldn't get in touch with anyone last night, but Ab fired off several e-mails to her counterparts there, and I have the phone numbers, of course. They open at nine." He glanced at his watch. "That's Eastern time . . . about forty minutes from now."

"This mean anything?" Dorry tapped a fingernail on the series of letters and numbers printed in the corner of the photograph.

Abby answered. "It's a coding format that most museums use. It's confusing because it's not universal within the international community . . . but what *is* universal with us, you know? It's like the metric system. America adopted it, but doesn't use it. We support the metric system every inch of the way." They all smiled. Continuing, Abby pointed and read, "Item 267—lot-4932881.pe.L/nfd. Here's what it means. The item number is its designator within a specific lot, or grouping . . . in this case, lot number 4932881."

"Okay," Dorry said.

"The *pe* is for *personal effects*. That lets us know that the object was part of a person's personal property. The number, 267, suggests that quite a bit of personal property was

collected from the life of this individual. That leads me to
believe that this was a person of some significance. You
know what I'm saying? I mean . . . to have so much of one
person's stuff."

"Good point," Dylan agreed.

"What does the *L* stand for?" Mark prompted.

"Loan," Abby replied. "It is an item available for loan.
The capital letter means that the piece is available for loan
to schools, private institutions . . . just about anyone who
will insure it. If a small *l* were in that spot, we would know
that the object was available only for loan to museums."

"Finally, the *nfd* means 'not for display.'" Abby squinted
and shrugged her shoulders slightly. "This probably means
that it has been set aside and is considered to be of lesser
importance. But when you think about it, 'of lesser importance' is a relative term. The Smithsonian owns 140 million
individual items."

"You're joking," Mark said.

"No, I'm not," she responded. "Can you imagine the
administrative load? The item identification, tagging,
restoration, maintenance . . . the number of people required
for an operation like they have is hard to comprehend!"

Dorry held the copy of the photo up and spoke to
Dylan. "Will we know *today* whose personal effects this
came from?"

"We'll know in thirty minutes."

⚛ ELEVEN

IT WAS ONLY A SNOWBALL. NOT PARTICULARLY
heavy, it was the approximate size and shape of a twelve-
year-old boy's hand. The throw itself, lobbed over the heads
of those gathered, was certainly not of significant strength
to provoke the reaction that followed. Its accuracy, however, was undeniable.

Perhaps it was a rock, or an oyster shell from the street,
that found its way into the packed wad of slushy ice, but
when it hit Matthew Kilroy just below the ear, the rage he
had kept in check for months was no longer controllable.
His rifle was already up. All he had to do was pull the trigger. And that is exactly what he did.

Hugh Montgomery, the man to Kilroy's right, was the
next to fire, discharging his weapon in concert with the
man to *his* right. With a suddenness roused by panic, every
man following the other, and in effect following no one,
the British soldiers fired fourteen muskets in a space of less
than five seconds, each finding its mark.

In the cold, still, late afternoon of March 5, the thick gunsmoke refused to rise. Instead it hung like an evil spirit over the carnage and lent an air of stunned illusion to the colonists, who, for the moment, couldn't believe what had happened, and the soldiers, who couldn't believe what they'd done.

Crispus Attucks had been the first to fall. A black man, Attucks had spent the last twenty years working whaling ships out of Boston. He crawled for a few feet before collapsing. Now he lay dead in the street with two musket balls deep in his chest. His eyes were still open, gazing sightlessly past the soldiers of the Twenty-ninth Regiment to the harbor, from which he would never sail again.

Samuel Gray, a rope maker, was killed while carrying a one-hundred-foot roll of finished hemp on his shoulder. He died instantly from the effects of a bullet that entered his head at the hairline, just forward of his temple.

Running at the first volley of shots, James Caldwell was cut down by two bullets in the back—proof enough to most that the British excuse of self-defense was a fabrication. Caldwell, a merchant seaman with a wife and child in Boston, died where he fell.

Patrick Carr, thirty years of age, worked as a maker of leather breeches in a shop on Queen Street. When the initial shot rang out, he covered a child with his body. Firing from the balcony of the Custom House, a soldier shot him in the hip. The lead traveled an unruly path through his body, exiting his right side. Carr died in his bed two weeks later.

Of the five who were killed, only Samuel Maverick was guilty of more than shouted words. He had actually thrown snowballs at the soldiers. A tall seventeen-year-old, he was an apprentice to Hiram Greenwood, an ivory turner, and should have been at work. He had disobeyed his mother's explicit instructions to stay well away from the Custom House on King Street where the British soldiers were barracked. Samuel's mother was a widow and depended on her only son for companionship and income. Samuel was mortally injured by a shot through his stomach. The musket ball was removed from his back, but he died in his mother's arms the following morning.

Six other men and boys were also severely wounded and being tended by the crowd that had gradually gathered its wits and was returning. Their rifles spent and seeking to avoid being hung immediately, the soldiers quickly retreated toward Custom House. They were intercepted by Benjamin Burdick, a Bostonian by birth, who walked directly up to the soldiers and spit at the feet of Thomas Preston, the captain of the Twenty-ninth. "I want only to see faces that I may swear to in front of God," Burdick said and spit again.

"Move along," Preston ordered. "This fight has ended."

"Remember this day, sir," Burdick responded. "This fight has just begun!"

And so it would be. For most of a decade, the cautious hospitality extended to the British by its American colonies had been rolling inexorably downhill. Encumbered by debt accrued during the French and Indian War, the king sought to balance Great Britain's accounts by using his "American children" as an income source.

The Stamp Act, passed by the British Parliament on March 22, 1765, was only one example of the king's strategy for plunder. This was a straightforward tax on newspapers, almanacs, wills, bills of sale, licenses, pamphlets—even playing cards and simple receipts! A constant parade of proclamations, acts, and decrees began to impose impossible financial burdens on businesses and families alike.

The colonial fury was not due to the amount of taxation the British were attempting to collect. Their anger revolved around the question of whether King George had the right to tax them at all. The power to levy taxes indiscriminately, they all agreed, was a power that might well be used to destroy them.

In response to growing unrest, the king openly used taxes to finance regiments of British infantry, moving them permanently into Boston neighborhoods for the "safety" of the local people. In February 1768, Samuel Adams of Massachusetts created a pamphlet urging the colonists to rebel against this "protection" and the taxation without representation, which succeeded in convincing the merchants of Massachusetts and New York to begin a boycott of all British items. Soon after, British warships arrived in Boston Harbor.

Philadelphia joined the boycott of British goods in March 1769, and in May, responding to a speech by George Washington, Virginia added itself to the list of colonies boycotting all things British. By October, that list had grown to include New Jersey, North Carolina, and Rhode Island. In response, King George sent additional troops.

When, at last, a regiment of soldiers—members of an unwanted occupying force—finally fired upon unarmed civilians, it was as inevitable as it was horrifying. Forever known as the Boston Massacre, the event became a touchstone—a rallying point—for a nation struggling with its own birth. Benjamin Burdick was correct in his assessment

of that moment's historical significance: The fight had
just begun.

PHILADELPHIA—JUNE 27, 1776

The older of the two men had closed his eyes in an
effort to fully concentrate as his friend's voice filled the
carriage, spilling out the open windows and mingling with
the sound of the horse's hooves striking the cobblestone
street. He frowned slightly and, as politely as he could manage, interrupted. "Stop right there. Brilliant, certainly . . .
and absolutely wonderful as it is . . . but if I may . . ."

Speaking carefully and with the utmost respect, he indicated a choice of words with which he disagreed. "There
at the beginning of the second paragraph . . . I concur that,
yes, truths *are* 'sacred and undeniable.' But, in my opinion,
the sentence cries out for a simpler, more forceful term."
He paused. "Try . . . *self-evident.*"

The younger man, reading the words he had so painstak-
ingly written, was seated with the pages balancing in his lap
as the carriage driver steered the horse over yet another very
large bump. He considered the suggestion for a moment,
then indicated his agreement with a grunt as he made a mental note to change the phrase. "Thank you, John," he said.
"Proceeding . . . I'll begin again with the second paragraph.

"We hold these truths to be self-evident, that all men are
created equal . . ." He glanced briefly at his friend who,
swaying in the seat facing him, nodded his acceptance of
the change, ". . . that they are endowed by their Creator
with certain unalienable Rights, that among these are Life,
Liberty, and the pursuit of Happiness.

"That to secure these rights, Governments are instituted among Men, deriving their just powers from the consent of the governed. That when any Form of Government becomes destructive of these ends, it is the right of the people to alter or abolish it, and to institute new Government, laying its foundation on such principles and organizing its powers in such form, as to them shall seem most likely to effect their Safety and Happiness.

"Prudence indeed, will dictate that Governments long established should not be changed for light and transient causes; and accordingly . . ."

The movement and hypnotic sounds of the horse-drawn carriage threatened to put John Adams to sleep. As he attempted to focus on the content of the younger man's writing, he nonetheless allowed his mind to close down. The crushing responsibility that had lately become his seemed to increase by the minute. He now served the Continental Congress on no less than twenty-six different committees—leading a third of those—and in the morning Adams would present to Congress a final draft of this statement, or declaration, that had been so beautifully composed by his young friend.

Adams opened his eyes briefly and studied the lanky figure reading aloud before him. Thomas Jefferson, only thirty-three years old, was the youngest of the delegates from Virginia. He was three inches over six feet tall, and his long legs folded uncomfortably into the coach. Jefferson's copper-colored hair and freckles made him conspicuous among the other members of Congress, who were generally older . . . and shorter.

By contrast, Adams, from Boston, was only five feet, seven inches in height. His round shape and balding head differed distinctly from the slim figure cut by the younger man. Adams, who consistently dressed in a plain manner, ignoring current fashions, was only forty years of age, but assumed by many to be much older.

Jefferson's contributions to this Second Congress had been, so far, unexceptional. He was not an outstanding speaker, excelling instead at presenting clear thoughts on the written page in a fiery and effective manner. It was this talent for lofty prose that landed him among the Committee of Five, as it was called, and tapped him specifically to draft a proclamation to state their position.

The Committee of Five consisted of Adams and Jefferson, Benjamin Franklin, Roger Sherman, and Robert Livingston. It had been assumed by Congress, when the appointments were made, that Adams would draft the document. He, however, had insisted on Jefferson. When the younger man questioned his decision, Adams had replied, "Because you write better than I do!" Subsequently, Adams and the others worked on the document as editorial advisors.

"... that these United colonies are, and of Right, ought to be Free and Independent States; that they are ..." Jefferson looked up. "Are you with me?"

Adams blinked. He cleared his throat and inhaled. Had he been asleep? He wasn't sure. "Yes. I apologize. Please continue."

The red-haired man found his place with a finger, then continued, "... that they are Absolved from all Allegiance to the British Crown, and that all political connection between them and the State of Great Britain, is and ought to be, totally dissolved ..."

The two men were as different as night and day. Their physical differences were obvious, but trifling compared to

their monetary holdings. Jefferson's family was exceedingly
wealthy and he had never cooked, cleaned, chopped wood,
or even saddled his own horse. Adams, the son of a farmer,
had grown up chopping wood and, even as a Boston attorney, continued to do so. But both men had become important to each other in an amazingly short period of time.
Adams was proud of Jefferson and considered him a pro-
tégé. Jefferson, for his part, saw Adams as a mentor. Clearly,
both felt a sense of destiny as they led the forging of a new
nation, and if either was ever haunted by doubts, no one
ever knew it. They did battle with those demons as effec-
tively as the men and women of the colonies were learning to do with the Redcoats.

The war had already begun. On the night of the eigh-
teenth of April, the year before, farmers and merchants,
warned with moments to spare by an engraver named
Revere, turned out to meet British troops who were
moving to destroy their military stores in Concord,
Massachusetts. A brief engagement on Lexington Green
was the first "shot heard 'round the world." Other skir-
mishes soon followed.

In Boston, on June 16, Adams' own eight-year-old son,
John Quincy, watched the Battle of Bunker Hill from atop
Penn's Hill on the family farm. Of the 2,400 red-clad British
soldiers, the 1,054 casualties inflicted by the colonists
accounted for 40 percent of their ranks. The American dead
and wounded numbered 441, including 30 who were captured during the retreat. The fight, though won by the
British, was a turning point in the minds of the colonists,
for it proved that the king's army was not unbeatable.

But the war was one thing. The Revolution, Adams
stated, had already been completed before the war was

begun, for the Revolution was in the minds and hearts of the people. The colonists had made difficult choices during this time. Choices not of self, but of a greater good. Adams' actions during the Stamp Act crisis was a case in point, discussed in private by many of the members of Congress who were in awe of his personal integrity.

The new law could have easily brought about Adams' ruin. The crux of the matter was this: The colonists refused to purchase stamped paper while the royal governor refused to acknowledge legal documents without the required stamps! And though this had the effect of cutting off Adams' income as an attorney, he stood with the colonists, in contrast to some "patriots" who made choices of sacrifice only when it did not affect their pocketbooks.

". . . and for the support of this Declaration, with a firm reliance on the protection of divine Providence, we mutually pledge to each other our Lives, our Fortunes and our Sacred Honor." Jefferson pursed his lips and looked to Adams, who smiled.

"Excellent, Thomas," he said. "And in the morning, I shall present it to our brothers as if my very life depends upon it."

As the carriage slowed to a stop, Jefferson snorted. "When this document is circulated with your name affixed, your very life *will* depend upon it . . . and mine as well."

As the men stepped down from the coach, Jefferson carefully folded the pages and placed them inside his coat pocket. "This way, John," he said and led his friend to the side door of a large house. Adams glanced around. This was the first time he had joined Jefferson at his residence and was suitably impressed. While most of the delegates stayed with relatives or roomed together in boardinghouses, the young Virginian had leased this two-room suite shortly after arriving on May 14.

Entering the parlor, Adams saw that it covered the entire second floor of this new brick home. Located on the southwest corner of Seventh Street and Market Avenue, the suite, to Adams' mind, was huge. Like the carriage, it was grand by his standards, though he suspected Jefferson found the accommodations rather ordinary.

Jefferson took Adams' coat and removed his own, remembering to take the pages from the pocket. He indicated a comfortable, high-backed chair near an open window to his friend. "Please be seated, John. Madeira?" he offered, knowing it to be Adams' favorite.

"Yes," Adams accepted, "and if you'll forgive my impertinence, have you also a pipeful of your precious Virginia tobacco?"

Jefferson laughed. "Of course." As he uncorked the wine, he gestured with his elbow toward a covered dish on the table next to Adams' chair. "Please avail yourself of my good fortune. Fill your pockets."

Adams loaded his pipe and accepted the glass from his friend. The sounds of the city ending its day drifted through the open window. Jefferson retrieved a portable lap desk from the dining table and, sitting in a chair near Adams, spread the pages out for both of them to see. "I have done my best."

"Is this absolutely your final draft?" Adams asked. "No more thoughts?"

Jefferson smiled. "Would you like me to read it again?" When Adams didn't reply, he answered his own question. "I thought not." He passed the pages to the older man and said, "Copy them then, in your own hand, and be ready for the morrow."

"What will happen tomorrow, Thomas?" Adams asked good-naturedly as he plucked a coal from the tinder pot, which was kept burning on the table next to the tobacco.

Jefferson leaned back with his glass and crossed his arms, waiting to answer until the older man had successfully lit his pipe. "You will be more spellbinding than any of the great orators. Cicero will be remembered as an amateur compared to the skills you will display. With your command of language and the rise and fall of your glorious voice, Congress will be eating out of your hand." He took a sip of the Madeira. "Then, of course, they will take what I have written and rip it to shreds."

Both men laughed heartily for they knew Jefferson's tongue-in-cheek prediction to be accurate indeed. No one approached Adams' ability as a speaker. And while Jefferson was a wordsmith, they also knew that Congress was likely to heavily edit what they had prepared.

"Ahh! I almost forgot to return your charm," Jefferson said suddenly as he reached for his lap desk, which had been placed on the floor, and opened it. Momentarily scratching through used quills and loose papers, he drew out a small, rectangular object. Scooped a bit on one side, it was reddish-brown and etched deeply. He passed it to Adams. "Tell me the story behind that again," he prompted.

Adams didn't immediately place it in his pocket, but turned it over in his hands, the better to view the side with the marks. "No story really," Adams said, never taking his eyes off the object. "It was my father's, and his before him. My great-great-grandfather, Henry Adams, brought this with him from England in 1638. Family legend has it once belonging to Joan of Arc. An Adams was a king's guard and received it as a gift from the maid before she was burned."

He sipped his wine and shifted in the chair, shrugging slightly. "That is the romantic tale, in any event."

Jefferson smiled. "Curious, certainly, wouldn't you say? First Joan of Arc . . . now us?"

"I must admit," Adams said, "if it is indeed true, the thought had occurred to me as well."

Jefferson pushed the notion again. "Pondering the message carved into your object's surface, knowing a bit about her quest . . . and now ours . . . the coincidence will most assuredly add to the family legend!" They sat quietly, each enjoying the other's company until Jefferson poured more Madeira and asked, "How did you come to translate the markings?"

Adams laughed suddenly. "Doth this enigma have you perplexed, Thomas?"

"No," Jefferson said somewhat defensively, "of course not! It is merely a novelty." Then, seeking to turn the tables, he said, "You, John, are the one who insisted I place it in my desk whilst drafting our Declaration. And you, sir," he continued with a teasing smile, "are the one who speaks to Congress with the rock in his pocket as a boy would carry his lucky piece!" Nodding once as if to say, *there!* Jefferson waited for his friend's reply.

"You are correct," Adams said, chuckling and exhibiting a degree of embarrassment. Then, in a quiet voice, he said, "But answer me truthfully, all riposte aside, do you not find it exceedingly odd?"

Jefferson sighed. "Yes, I do. And a second time, John, how did you come to translate the markings?"

Before speaking, Adams noticed his pipe had gone out and indicated the bowl of tobacco nearby. "May I?" he asked.

"Certainly."

Jefferson waited patiently as his friend turned and opened the bowl. Packing the pipe full of the aromatic tobacco, Adams said, "It is Aramaic. Did I already tell you this?"

"No."

"Aramaic is an ancient language similar to Latin."

"I am familiar with Aramaic," Jefferson said. "Phrases of Aramaic are often blended with the ancient Greek and Hebrew texts."

"Exactly!" Adams agreed. Then, as an aside, he asked, "Did you study Greek and Hebrew?"

"With passion," he responded. "While a student at the College of William and Mary, my language professors were uncommonly strident on the subject of ancient texts. Aramaic, however, was not among them."

Adams sat back down and lit his pipe. "When I was accepted to Harvard, I was already fluent in several languages." Jefferson sipped the Madeira and listened. He did not express surprise at the degree of education to which Adams had been exposed, for this was the norm, not the exception. "By my third year I, too, became steeped in ancient texts and came upon a passage one day, tucked amidst the Hebrew, that reminded me of my father's charm. A professor identified the excerpt as Aramaic, and when I brought the piece in one day, he helped me translate it."

Jefferson reached over and picked up the object, which Adams had laid on a small table between them. He touched the etching with his knuckle. "Extraordinary. The people shall be free, you say?"

Adams puffed on his pipe. "*By your hand,* the people shall be free. *By your hand,* I am quite sure, is the message."

"How so?"

Adams tilted his head toward Jefferson. "Do you believe in charms?"

"Decidedly not."

"Nor do I. *Charm* was my father's word, not my own." He studied the pipe, making sure it was lit, then continued. "There is no such thing as 'lucky' and items carried for luck are extra weight in the pocket of a fool. Consider the moronic rabble who carry a rabbit's foot for luck, never pausing to consider the lack of protection it provided its original owner!" Jefferson chuckled.

"In any case," Adams said, "I *do* believe that words, paintings, a statue, or an object can harbor within it the unique power to inspire. And when one is inspired, an action is often taken. Only actions will change the world, Thomas. Intentions will not. Words will not. Only direct action *by your hand*, will ever change anything.

"There are those who would say, 'Let us be patient. Let us sit and wait upon the Almighty.' I say to them, 'Get up! The Almighty is waiting on you!' Make no mistake, the Lord God instructs us; He leads us and inspires us, but He expects us to *do something* with the gifts we've been given. It is a choice that too few make.

"Examine the markings on the object. They are mere words and have no more power than my pipe! But they inspire me to a choice—me, one man among the entire world's population. The choice to *do something*. And the action that one man takes, I believe, changes everything for everyone.

"This object? I have no idea what it is, what it is made of, or its origin. If indeed, it was borne by Joan of Arc, you can be certain that she understood its true meaning. History tells us that. This was a girl who did not set the object on a fence post and wait nervously for someone else to do what needed to be done. She sensed the inspiration, accepted the responsibility, and determined that, 'By all that is holy, by *my* hand, these people shall be free!'

"Thomas, this is why I left the object with you. By your hand, the people shall be free. As you composed the declaration whose words will ring through the ages, I wanted you inspired—so that you might inspire. I wanted your heart's lifeblood poured out upon the pages. It is not enough that we merely know the right thing to do. We must *do* it!"

Adams straightened his posture and inhaled deeply. "Excuse me, Thomas. I apologize. On this subject, I am rather easily carried away."

Jefferson reached out a hand and touched Adams on the shoulder. "No need to apologize, my friend. Carry that passion with you on the morrow. Another glass?"

"No," Adams said, rising. "I have other committee work to accomplish, a letter to Abigail overdue, and," he said, patting the pages inside his coat pocket, "I must prepare this."

As Jefferson walked his friend to the door, Adams turned. "One more thing, Thomas, if it is not an inconvenience."

"None at all," Jefferson said, stopping for a moment.

Adams ran his hand over his balding head. "Thomas . . ." He paused.

"Is something wrong, John?" Jefferson asked, a concerned expression on his face.

Adams spoke. "I wish that you not see my query as personal, but as a matter of direction for our nation . . ."

"Go ahead," Jefferson said guardedly. "What is it?"

"Do you truly believe that—how did you put it?—'all men are created equal'?"

"Of course."

Adams let his friend's answer hang in the air for a moment, then said, "Excellent. Well, then, consider the words. Good evening," and he turned to go.

"Wait," Jefferson said, stopping him. "You're speaking of my slaves." Adams said nothing. "John, you know how I feel about slavery. I am against it. I've written and published papers on the subject!"

Adams slowly nodded. "Yet you own them still, Thomas."

Jefferson appeared anguished. "My intentions, however—"

Adams held up his hand to cut him off. "By your hand, the people shall be free—or not. Thomas, you will always be my friend. But I fear that a passion for liberty cannot possibly be as strong in the breasts of those who become accustomed to depriving their fellow creatures of theirs. It is a choice, Thomas, and one that history will record."

ONLY A FEW DAYS LATER, THE OFFICIAL DOCUMENT— the Declaration of Independence—was signed. There was no special recognition of the moment, no ceremony, merely a room full of men doing what they believed to be right and true. As each name was affixed to the page, the men were aware that defeat was not an option. If the war were to be lost, the owners of names so prominently displayed would most assuredly be hunted down and executed as traitors to the crown.

For the most part, all fifty-six signers of the document felt the tug of history as they "pledged their lives, their fortunes, and their sacred honor." Only the signature of Stephen Hopkins from Rhode Island showed any evidence of a quaking hand. He had long endured severe palsy and signed his name using his left hand to guide his right. On completion of the letters to his name, Hopkins straightened himself and said, "Gentlemen! My hand trembles. My heart does not."

John Adams went on to serve the young nation as the second president of the United States of America. Thomas Jefferson was elected president following Adams. They remained friends though they did not always agree—and as history records, more often than not, this was the case. Their lives, however, were intertwined by destiny. Two men, brought together for a moment that changed the world.

Many years later, on Friday, June 30, 1826, several of Boston's leaders made their way to nearby Braintree to visit the ailing ex-president. Adams was in his library, seated in his favorite chair. In four days, he was told, the nation would celebrate its fiftieth anniversary—fifty years to the day from which the Declaration of Independence was ratified. Would he, they wondered, offer a toast to be presented to the huge crowds that were expected? Without hesitation, the old man raised his voice and said, "Independence forever!" When asked if there was anything else he would care to add, Adams smiled. "Not a word," was his response.

On that evening, July 4, the Adams children and grandchildren gathered around the great man's bedside and listened with him as the cheers and happy explosions of fireworks resounded throughout the city. His heart stopped at 6:20. John Adams was 90 years, 247 days old. His last words were, "Thomas Jefferson survives." But Jefferson had died three hours earlier.

❊ TWELVE

AN HOUR AFTER THEIR EARLY MORNING BREAK-
fast, they were all in Dylan's office as he finished his call to
the Smithsonian. Abby had pulled the folding chair from
behind the door and was seated facing Dylan. Mark, his
hands stuffed in his pockets, listened in silence with his
back against the closed door while Dorry, on her knees at
Dylan's desk, scribbled questions and ideas on a notepad as
they all listened to one side of the conversation.

From his swivel chair, Dylan was enjoying the reactions
of the others as he repeated the facts given to him over the
phone. "Yes," he said in conclusion. "We'll e-mail our
museum's ID codes, address, UPS account numbers . . . You'll
get everything within the hour . . . Yes, please overnight it.
And Don, one more thing, would it be possible for you to
include the Quincy letter with that item? . . . Great. Thanks
so much. Listen, anything you ever need on this end, let me
know. Take care."

Dylan reached across the desk, replacing the handset in

its cradle, and then spun his chair in a full circle. "Yeow!" he exulted. "What do you think about that?!"

"Adams *and* Adams," Dorry said, still writing. "It's incredible. I wish I remembered more history, but I'll look all this up."

Mark spoke. "I think we all got everything he said. By the way, your guy is still running the computer, right?"

"Oh, yeah. It runs 24/7. Even when he's gone."

"We need to meet again tonight, don't we?" Mark asked the group in general.

"Yes," Dorry answered. "Definitely."

Abby stifled a yawn. "I'm up for it," she said, "but I have to get some sleep at some point."

Dylan glanced at the clock on his desk. "I say we go till lunch, head home to sleep, then over to Mark and Dorry's . . ." Catching Abby's "look" and realizing he had just invited himself over to their house, Dylan quickly apologized. "I'm sorry. That was rude. Will it be okay to meet at your house?"

Dorry smiled and waved off the apology. "No problem; our place is fine. That'll make it easier on me."

"Great! I'll want to come by here before we head your way. I can check on Perasi. Who knows? We might get some up-to-the-minute stuff." He paused, thinking carefully, then said, "I'm also going to call Don back at the Smithsonian. Obviously, he'll still have to overnight the relic, but I want to see if he'll fax or e-mail me the letter from John Quincy Adams. Then we'll have it for tonight."

They waited patiently while Dylan punched the numbers into his desk phone, then talked briefly with his back to them. Within seconds, he hung up and swung his chair back around. "He's already out of his office. I left a message on his voice mail. I'm sure it won't be any problem."

"Did the guy . . . Don, right?" Abby asked. "Did he read any of the letter to you?"

"Naw. He said it was pretty long and is about John Quincy Adams turning the object over to the collection of his father's personal items. Don said he found the letter when he ran his own in-house search for the object. Evidently, the letter is a part of the Quincy Adams grouping—anyway, I think we'll have a copy of it tonight."

"Yeah," Mark said, "I'm curious about that whole thing. So . . . what time tonight?"

Dorry broke in. "You guys just come on over when you wake up. I'll have food, so no need to stop on the way." Then to Dylan she said, "Can I hang here until you two leave? I don't have anything pressing at the *Post,* and I'd like to meet Perasi, see the computer . . . you know?"

"Sure," Dylan said. "The way this is unfolding, well, it'd be a heck of an article, huh?"

"Don't think that hasn't crossed my mind," Dorry said, "but right now, I feel as though I've been reading the world's greatest mystery and someone has torn out the pages of the last chapter!"

DORRY WALKED INTO THE LIVING ROOM TO PLACE A tray of taco shells on the table and saw the headlights of Dylan's car as it turned into the driveway. She waited at the door and, as he and Abby walked up, ushered them inside. They looked much better, Dorry noticed, than they had earlier. Fresher, cleaner, both wore jeans and sweatshirts. Dylan had a medium-size cardboard box in his hands. "I slept. I showered," Abby said as she gave Dorry a quick hug.

"Hey, tacos!" Dylan said as he moved toward the table.

"Yessir," Dorry said. "My finest meal. You guys make yourselves at home—drinks in the kitchen—let me get Michael settled. Mark will be right in."

"Hi, guys," Mark said from the kitchen. "You both look . . . awake. Dorry won't be long. Coke? Coffee? Green Kool-Aid? Whadaya want?" Abby and Dylan joined him there as he poured soft drinks, making small talk while they waited.

A few minutes later, Dorry joined the group and flopped into a chair at the table. "Whew!" she said. "Michael is a handful. Okay, let's eat." She took hold of the armrests on the chair and started to pull herself up again, but was stopped by Dylan.

"Hang on, Dorry," he said. "You want to see what we have before we eat?"

"Actually, yes, but I thought you would be hungry."

Dylan grinned. "Forget the food for a minute. Mark, get Dorry some coffee. She'll want to be awake for this."

When Dorry had her cup, they all settled forward, elbows on the table, and Dylan began. "You first? Or me first?" he asked Abby.

"You go," she said. "Start with the letter." Then to Mark and Dorry, she added, "I will give you the measurements from the radio scope after he's finished."

Dylan began by opening the cardboard box he had placed on the floor beside his chair. Removing the page on top, the Chandlers could see that it was a faxed copy of what they assumed to be the letter from John Quincy Adams. "We'll have the original in our hands tomorrow,"

Dylan said, "but for our purposes, this is just as good. We won't be testing paper or anything like that. It's the letter's content that is important. And the content is . . . well . . ." He glanced at Abby who smiled and pretended to shiver, "Let's just say the content of this letter confirms some of what we already know and creates a few more possibilities. It is addressed to the 'Committee of Presidential Archives.'" He passed the page to Mark. "Here. Read it aloud."

Mark took it and saw that the handwriting was beautiful and flowing. The letter had been written on stationery with an *A* printed at the top of the page in an old, swirling style. The date, handwritten in the top right corner, was December 27, 1847.

Dear Sirs,

I trust this missive to find you healthy and of good cheer as we seek together yet another new year. Endeavoring to depart this earth with as firm a foundation erected for the legacy of my father, John Adams, I humbly submit this personal heirloom to your trust as belonging to his effects, more certainly than my own.

On the evening of his passing, goaded merely by impulse, I plucked it from his bedside as a remembrance of him. Unimpressive though the object may seem, family history insists upon it once belonging to Jeanne d'Arc. Nevertheless, my grandfather, five generations removed, brought the object from Somerset in 1638. From him, or at least from that point, it passed from father to son until it was possessed by my father.

The markings visible on the object are Aramaic. Translated by him as a young man, they read, "By your hand, the people shall be free." Knowing these words, knowing how fervently my father believed them to be true, and being aware of the part he played in the founding of our nation, I considered the item a remembrance of my personal heritage—much the same as another child might view his father's pocketknife or timepiece. In any case, I have carried it with me during my life, as did my father.

Incidentally, my surviving son, Charles, initiated this action that I am presently undertaking, for he is of the opinion that the item not be placed upon his shelf or in his pocket as was my intention, but entrusted into your care as a personal item of the second president of these United States.

One final point. Aware as I am of my own advanced age and declining health, it is incumbent upon me to bow to the importance of written record. I am hesitant to include the following observation for it has no basis in hard fact or historical meaning. My next words delve rather deeply into impression and perception— and for that, I beg you forgive an old man. I will strive to convey this occurrence in a factual manner and avoid the slack-jawed wonder by which I remember it.

As I noted earlier, this object of my father's has been carried on my person, until this day, for more than twenty-one years. Always in the high

right pocket of my coat. Often, as I walked the halls of government, the item's translation sprang to mind, but other than my wife and children, to my certain knowledge, no one understood the markings and further, no other person held the object—save two—and both these exceptions occurred on the same day.

As you are aware, I ended my self-imposed retirement twelve full years after my presidency ended in order to appear as an attorney before our nation's Supreme Court. My defense of the Africans aboard the slave schooner *Amistad* was successful, but as the official pronouncement of "not guilty" was made on March 9, 1841, one of the strangest events in my life took place.

Chief Justice Marshall declared the slaves to be at liberty and directed that they be returned to their homeland. At that moment, Cinque, the man who had led the *Amistad* revolt, looked to me for confirmation that he was indeed, now free, and plainly asked, in English, "May I see the stone?" At first, I did not understand, but again, he asked, then tapped my pocket with his hand. I removed the object. Cinque took it in his hand and kissed it.

Many people in the courtroom witnessed this brief exchange. One other attorney, however, Francis Scott Key of the District of Columbia, an ally of mine in the defense, gently removed it from Cinque's hand and sat down. As I continued to receive the medley of congratulation and threat a case of this sort generates, I watched Key from the corner of my eye. For a quarter of an hour, he alternately stared at the object and looked away as if seeking to remember a forgotten name.

In due course, I retrieved the item and made my way home. I later asked Key about this strange encounter. He said only that the object struck him as "vastly familiar." As for Cinque, I only encountered him on one other occasion and never came to understand his fervor for the object, nor how he even knew it was in my pocket.

In closing, I must once again apologize for the stirring of fact and fancy with which I have presented this item. It is now, however, in your keeping, for our nation, in the memory of my dear father.

I am most sincerely yours,

John Quincy Adams

Mark studied the signature briefly, then exhaled loudly as he lowered the page. He opened his mouth as if to say something, closing it almost as suddenly. "I'm having a hard time putting this together."

"Isn't this the most exciting—," Abby stammered. "Is this unbelievable?"

"Yeah, it's unbelievable," Dylan said, "but I'm with Mark. The whole picture has not emerged for me yet. It's as confusing as it is exciting. And wait till you see the rest of this. Right now, you aren't confused at all!"

As always, Dorry was taking notes. She paused, flipped a few pages in her book, and said, "Here's some background I did this afternoon. John Adams was the second president.

Quincy was number six. Quincy was the first president to be fathered by a president. By the way, of the first seven presidents, John Adams was the only one to have a male heir." She looked up. "That doesn't really mean anything. I just thought it was interesting.

"Of the founding fathers—Franklin, Washington, Jefferson, Patrick Henry—John Adams was one of the very few who never owned a slave. And his family never owned slaves. That's curious, isn't it? Considering the translation on the object."

Dylan interrupted. "Hey! What do you make of them *knowing* what it said? They translated it!"

"Yeah," Mark said. "And Francis Scott Key in the letter? He only wrote 'The Star Spangled Banner.' And *Amistad?*"

"Did you see *that* movie?" Abby asked Mark.

"Yes, and do you know who made that movie?"

"Spielberg!" they practically shouted at once.

"Holy moly," Dylan said. "We have a picture of Schindler with one of these things. Now it's connected to the guy from the *Amistad.* You know, I have Spielberg's phone number. I think I'll call and ask if he knows what's going on!"

"Guys." Mark's serious tone cut through the teasing. "Dorry"—he motioned with his hand—"I need a piece of paper and the pen." As she slid the items within his reach, Mark quickly divided the blank page in front of him into three columns and at the top, labeled them *Live, Fed,* and *Free.* "Have you noticed this?" he said, talking as he wrote.

"We thought it was coincidence . . . neat . . . strange, whatever, that George Washington Carver, who did so much with food . . . had the food stone." In the *Fed* column, Mark wrote *Carver.* "Now, we have John Adams . . ."

"Oh, man, I see where you're going with this," Dylan broke in.

"Hang on," Mark said. "Slow down. Let's do this carefully. Let's put every piece of this puzzle on the table . . ."

"Oh, man man man!" Dylan rattled. "You don't even know what I have in the—"

"Dylan! Hang on, brother! We have to lay this out precisely."

"You have to understand, Dylan," Dorry interrupted. "It's the detective thing. Slooow . . . steeeady . . . there might be a fingerprint on that blade of grass two miles from the crime scene."

Ignoring her, Mark continued, "In the *Free* column, we put Adams . . . Adams . . . Joan of Arc . . ."

"Francis Scott Key," Abby said.

"Yeah," Mark agreed, writing slowly. "Francis Scott Key . . . Who else?" Mark asked.

"The *Amistad* guy goes in that column too," Dylan said. "And put Henry Wallace and Norman Borlaug in the *Fed* column."

"Patterson," Dorry said. "The president of Carver's college. Frederick Patterson. Put him down."

"And in the *Live* column?" Mark asked the others. "This is just an assumption, of course, but an obvious one . . ."

"Schindler," they answered.

"My gosh," Abby continued to talk. "See how this is lining up? Perasi found some more matches too. And I have to tell you about the scopes."

Mark shook his head. "This is so weird."

Dylan pulled the last two pages from the box and laid them side by side. "For you, my friend," he smiled. "It just got weirder."

Dorry stood over Mark's shoulder with her coffee in hand as they studied the two images before them, recognizing neither. "Perasi does good work, doesn't he?" Dylan asked as he pushed a page forward. "Look at this one first."

It was a photograph of a bookish man in a white lab coat with which he wore a black tie. His receding hairline and thick, black-rimmed glasses gave the appearance of an older person, though his lack of wrinkles and the twinkle in his eye revealed the truth that he was, indeed, still a young man. He posed in the picture with a microscope, but to his right, sitting directly on top of a stack of three books, was a relic. "Know him?" Dylan asked. Mark and Dorry shook their heads. "Tell 'em, Ab."

"Jonas Salk."

"No way!" Dorry said, picking up the page to get a closer look. "He discovered the polio vaccine. There's the object, right there."

"That's *Live*," Mark said.

"What?"

"*Live*. Jonas Salk. The polio vaccine. That object has got to be 'By your hand, the people shall live.' And"—Mark paused to look carefully at his wife—"if that is *Live*, and considering how these others are lining up, I have no doubt that it is, the relic Michael found in the creek."

For a moment they just looked at each other, lost in questions their minds were having trouble formulating, never mind answering. Dorry broke the silence. "Ab, when was that picture taken?"

Abby glanced at her notes. "May 5, 1955. Perasi found this one in the *Time* magazine microfilm. Salk died in '95. He was seventy when he died, so . . . he's thirty in this picture."

Addressing the image of the young doctor, Dorry asked, "Where did you get this? And who had it after you? Or did anybody?" She looked at Mark. "And how in the world did it end up in our backyard?"

"Check this guy out." Dylan changed the subject by picking up the other page. "Scary boy, isn't he?" The image was of a painting, and though it was the second to be shown, it had been the first to catch the eye of both Mark and Dorry when Dylan had laid them on the table a few minutes before. As they had examined the photograph and talked about Jonas Salk, the Chandlers' attention had continued to drift toward this image.

It was a painting of a male face from the shoulders up. The only word to describe the man was "terrifying." His black hair was wild with colored streaks of white and red. The skin on one side of his face was painted blue, the other bright yellow. He was screaming furiously as if he might lunge from the canvas. But the most incredible sight was the relic, front and center in the image, tied directly to the man's forehead.

"Geez! Who is that?" Dorry asked. "I'll have nightmares!"

"Date: 1304?" Dylan prompted.

Mark and Dorry shook their heads.

"'William Wallace,'" Abby read. "'Hero of Scotland. During a time in world history when the average male height was just over five feet, William Wallace stood six feet seven inches tall and possessed a physique to match. His sword'—which by the way, is on display today . . . where is that?" She turned the pages. "I have it on another sheet . . . okay, here. 'The sword, sixty-six inches in length and weighing almost nine pounds, can be seen at the Patrons of Cowanes Hospital in Scotland.

"'Wallace was obsessed by the idea of freedom for his

people and'—get this—," Abby interjected. She began to read
slowly. "'He often wore his "stone of destiny" into battle! He
was captured and executed in 1305, an event regarded by
many to have created an even greater clamor for freedom by
the people of Scotland.'" Abby closed her notebook.

Dorry checked what she had written. "Wallace was
1305. Joan of Arc . . . 1431. The first date we have on an
Adams is 1638 when the object came to America." She
paused, lost in thought. Suddenly, Dorry asked, "We *do* all
agree, don't we, that this lineup—Wallace, Joan of Arc,
Adams—this is all the same object, right? *Free?*"

"Yes," they concurred.

"Heck of a lineup," Dorry murmured and looked again
to her notes. "Abby," Dylan said. "What about the radio
scope?"

"Oh!" Abby shook her head as if waking up. "I almost
forgot." Opening her notebook again, Abby glanced at it,
then began. "You know the scope works by light refrac-
tion. I can see inside—shapes, stresses. Long story short, the
pieces *were* hollow in their original form, and the pressure
closures on the ends were immediate. A catastrophic event.

"I want to run the scope on the Adams piece coming in
tomorrow, because the picture of it, well, the shape is
somewhat different."

"You said a catastrophic event," Mark pointed out. "Any
idea what the catalyst might have been?"

Abby frowned. "What do you mean?"

"In my line of work," Mark explained, "the catalyst of a
catastrophic event would be a gun, a knife, a bomb, a car
bumper . . ."

"Okay, I gotcha. Well, rule out gun, bomb, and car
bumper." Mark smiled at Abby's remark. She continued.

"But I guess 'knife' is a possibility. It would have been a *big* knife . . . weight behind it, like a sword or an ax.

"Here's something peculiar. You can't see this with the naked eye, but with scope magnification and resolution, there appears to be edge-to-edge closure, caused by the catastrophic event, on both sides of the *Live* object. It's as if a Ziploc bag had a Ziploc on each end of the bag . . . are you following me? Two edges?" Everyone nodded, concentrating deeply on Abby's words.

"The food stone, however, has edge-to-edge closure on only one side. On the side opposite the pressure closure on the food stone, it is obvious that the original casting created its own hollow curve. On that end, there exists a rough spot about the size of a dime. In my opinion, something was attached, at some point, to that location on the food stone."

Changing the subject, Abby asked Dorry, "Are you getting anything from your sources?"

Dorry shook her head disgustedly. "Zip. Nada."

"Me neither," Mark said. "A lot of people had their hands on these things, but it looks like nobody ever stole one!" They all chuckled.

"Okay, here's what I'm doing next," Abby said. "The Adams piece comes in tomorrow. I'll scope it here, but here's some big news, I think. I checked around. I have a buddy I graduated with—undergrad—and after doing all his doctoral work, he went the extreme research route. That means University of Wisconsin–Madison. They are the big leagues.

"Among other things, they do chemical analysis of archaeological materials. They are among the only locations in the world with the instruments to tell us more. If everyone agrees, I have already given Perry a heads up and we can ship the three objects to him tomorrow afternoon. He has reserved time with a machine called an Inductively Coupled Plasma Atomic Emission Spectrometer."

Mark's eyes widened. "O-kaaaay . . ."

Abby laughed. "It's a mouthful. But Perry will be able to send me the results I want on computer models by e-mail. I want him to do two specific things. I want to examine those edges more closely than I can here and . . . I want to regressively age the edges."

Dorry looked at Mark. "That's what you do, right? With pictures of kids?"

He nodded. In work with missing persons, it was a common tactic to regress the picture of an adult in order to see if he or she is, in fact, the child that was lost years earlier.

"So, I want a regression of all three objects. I want a better idea of what these edges used to look like."

For a moment everyone was still. Then Dylan said, "Tell 'em why, Ab."

She hesitated, then lifted her chin. "I think they used to fit together," she said. "I think they are all pieces of something else."

Dorry leaned forward and put her face down on the table, cradled by her arms. Then, just as quickly, looked up. "I believe it," she stated, acceptance on her face. "I'm kinda blown away by the idea, but I think that has been bothering me too. It's all just . . . just too connected . . . for this not to have been, well . . . connected." She exhaled loudly and slumped back into her chair.

"Okay, then . . ." Mark spoke slowly. He was doodling with his pen on the piece of paper in front of him. "I have a question for you. If these pieces all fit . . ." He put down the pen and looked up. "Do we have all the pieces? Or are there more?"

❧ THIRTEEN

NEW YORK CITY—MAY 1, 1915

AT TEN O'CLOCK IN THE MORNING, THE TEMPERA-
ture was still unseasonably cool. The low clouds and driz-
zling mist seemed more suited for December or January
than the first day of May. Nigel Bailey waited patiently
under the canopy of Baron's Pub on Sixth Avenue, smoking a cigarette. He had called in quite a few markers from
friends—and friends of friends—to make this day happen.
If the meeting went well, he would be a rich man.

Bailey was of average height and compact build with
broad shoulders that hinted of an uncommon strength. His
complexion was dark, as were his eyes, and he sported a
bushy mustache that was longer than the hair on his head,
which was concealed, in any case, by a tall, beaver-skin hat.
Noticing his cigarette had burned almost to his fingertips,
Nigel quickly rolled another one and lit it from the last
flicker of the first. He was thirty-four years old and a world
traveler, though this was his first trip to America. Having
grown up in Australia, and on his own from the time he

was fourteen, he had made his way as a stock herder in the outback until leaving the country for good at twenty-three.

For a number of years, Nigel worked as a deckhand, mate, and finally purser on cargo and passenger vessels trading from Africa to European ports. It was on such a trip two years earlier that Nigel had first heard of the incredible discoveries being made in Egypt. The Valley of the Kings, as it was being called, was yielding its priceless treasures to one fool or another on almost a monthly basis. In Italy, the same thing was happening. Roman vaults and catacombs of long-buried dead were beginning to be found.

In the seaport of Venice, Nigel spent a month's wages in one evening, satisfying the thirst of a passenger who claimed to know the location of one such place. Prodigious amounts of the most expensive liquor finally managed to pry the secret from the man. The very next day Nigel left the employ of his captain.

The location turned out to be bogus—the drunken boasting of a determined storyteller. The search to that place, however, pointed to stepping-stones of more and better information, leading Nigel on an extended journey of months and miles, which finally, and quite by chance, bore fruit.

Nigel had worked throughout Spain and Italy, mostly as a woodcutter, earning enough money to pay his modest living expenses. One day, searching for hardwood on the estate of a wine producer, he happened upon a series of mounds. Having read newspaper descriptions of burial sites that had been located and unearthed, Nigel knew that, often, the only evidence of a tomb's existence was a small hill which sprang from otherwise level ground. Despite the realization that he was on private property, he ignored the possibility of imprisonment—Italy had already enacted strong legislation regarding the opening of ancient graves without government supervision—set aside his ax, and picked up a shovel.

There were five mounds, and it had taken him a full day to penetrate the first two. What he found in each was a single skeleton, fully formed, and fitted with a breastplate. A spearhead made of some kind of metal lay near both skeletons' heads. Nigel assumed the spear's shafts would have been wooden, thus decaying long ago. Both burial sites were empty except for the warriors who were laid directly onto the stone floor.

Studying the layout of the mounds, Nigel saw that he had opened two of the four graves that surrounded the one in the center. Mentally connecting the soldiers with the arrangement of the five mounds, and wondering what, if anything, they were guarding, Nigel dug into the side of the center mound and was rewarded for his effort.

When he had entered the tomb of Constantine XI, he did so on his knees. The single candle Nigel held flickered as the stale air brushed his face. At first, he had been disappointed. Parchment scrolls that turned to dust when he picked them up, several cracked vases, and some wooden carvings were all he noticed at first glance. No stacks of gold or silver. No diamonds or jewels.

The bones of the emperor were laid on a stone slab at the back of the tomb. The flesh had long since disappeared. The thumb of the emperor's right hand yielded a ring of gold, decorated with a green stone of some sort. On his left hand, which had separated into a pile of tiny bones as it was moved, there were three more rings of similar design. Nigel almost missed the medallion, dull and sifted with powdered human tissue, that was lying inside the chest cavity.

He reached through the rib bones to draw out the disk. It had evidently been worn on the great man's chest and, over the years, gradually fallen through the decaying body.

As he pulled it into the candlelight, Nigel had seen a hole that had been drilled into one side with a leather strap run through it. At least he thought it was leather. Whatever it *had* been was now reduced to dark, disintegrated pieces that had wound up and over the ribs, across the collarbone, around the base of the skull, and back down the other side.

Nigel brushed the remnants of the strap from the medallion and blew a final piece from the hole. Tucking it into his pocket with the rings, he opened a cloth sack, which he proceeded to fill with every other loose item in the tomb.

Nigel looked at his pocket watch as he threw his cigarette into the street. *Now to sell the lot,* he thought, as he spotted a black coach easing to a stop in front of the pub. Pulled by four matching horses, also black, the coach was magnificent, trimmed in gold with red leather accent. The driver opened the side door and offered a hand to the man Nigel had come to America to see.

Alfred Vanderbilt stepped out of the coach and straightened. Tall and elegant, he wore a pink carnation in the buttonhole of his knee-length, charcoal-gray, pinstriped jacket. Matching trousers, black lambskin gloves, and a silk-banded top hat completed the fashionable ensemble. Vanderbilt stepped aside as his personal valet, Ronald Denyer, followed him from the coach. Finally, two other men, one after the other, emerged in the coach's doorway and stepped to the street.

Nigel watched from the pub's entrance as one of the world's wealthiest men approached.

He had done his research well and knew Vanderbilt to

be a student of art and antiquities, a hobby on which he spent money lavishly. And he had the money to spend. Only thirty-eight years old, Alfred had already inherited the bulk of the Vanderbilt estate. Upon their father's death, each of his brothers and sisters—some younger, some older—had been willed seven million dollars. Alfred received seventy-six million.

While Vanderbilt was immediately recognized everywhere he went, he was also well respected. He was known to be a kind man and was not considered one of the robber barons—men who used their wealth as a weapon and, with it, bludgeoned the poor. It was common knowledge that, as a young man, Alfred alone among his siblings had insisted on beginning his business experience by "starting at the bottom" as a clerk in one of his father's offices. The public never forgot it. Neither did his father, as was evidenced by the division of his wealth.

"Mr. Vanderbilt!" Nigel called as he stepped to the curb with his hand outstretched. "Nigel Bailey, sir."

Vanderbilt expertly shucked his gloves and shook the man's hand. "Pleased to make your acquaintance, Mr. Bailey," he said. "Please meet my valet. This is Mr. Denyer." Nigel shook the hand of the shorter man, who was dressed well, though not so handsomely as his employer.

Then Vanderbilt introduced the other two men who were standing to the side in simple, dark suits. "These gentlemen are Drs. Osborn and Tate. Dr. Henry Fairfield Osborn, Director, and Dr. Lawrence Hardy Tate, Curator, of the American Museum of Natural History on Seventy-seventh Street." Nigel shook hands with both. "Shall we?" Vanderbilt asked, indicating the pub's entrance with a sweep of his arm as his valet hurried to open the door.

As Nigel followed the group into the restaurant, his mind raced. He hadn't counted on the presence of experts. Especially ones who might question his methods, which Nigel admitted were amateurish at best. *No worries,* he thought, *I'll bluster my way through.*

Inside, the waiters scurried to seat the Vanderbilt party at a round table beside the front window. Alfred and Nigel sat down and shifted their chairs a bit toward each other while the valet and Drs. Osborn and Tate discreetly took positions to the side. Not close enough to the lunch hour, Vanderbilt ordered only hot beverages for the table, which were delivered at once. Alone for the time being, Vanderbilt addressed his guest. "Mr. Bailey! My attorney tells me you are a recent arrival on our shores."

"Yes, sir. Only two weeks ago. Tramp steamer from Genoa." Nigel noticed that the valet, Ronald Denyer, was standing, circling the table and pouring the tea and coffee. *Cripes,* he thought, *this is a different life. This man has his own personal waiter!*

"The accent . . . Australian, am I correct?" Vanderbilt inquired.

"Yeah, right," Nigel grinned. "Down under. Ever been?"

"Several times, actually," Vanderbilt responded. "Lovely people with a spirit much the same as our own." He cleared his throat. "It is not my intention to rush you, Mr. Bailey. I am interested in your presentation. My attorney has filled me in on your efforts in a general way. I am, however, on a rather tight schedule. I'm booked for passage to Europe this afternoon. In fact, we leave for the port from here."

"No worries. Where would you like me to begin?"

"How about with the location of the tomb," Vanderbilt said congenially. "Where is it exactly?"

"Exactly, eh?" Nigel said innocently. "Yeah. I was prepared to give you the tomb's general location—that being
the continent of Europe—but you want me to tell you the
tomb's exact location. All right . . . the tomb's exact location is Italy."

Vanderbilt laughed and winked at his valet. "Point taken,
Mr. Bailey. Do answer this question though: How do you
know that the tomb you raided—"

"*Explored* would be a much nicer choice of words, Mr.
Vanderbilt," Nigel interrupted with a thoughtful expression on his face. "*Raided* is one of those terms that gets me
in trouble with the law"—he shot a knowing look at
Osborn—"and the items removed from your museum."

"Let me phrase it your way, then," Vanderbilt began
again. "How do you know that the tomb you 'explored'
was that of . . . Constantine, I believe I was told?"

"Because the bones were lying on a slab that was
engraved with his bloody name on it! I'll admit, I'm not
the brightest lad you'll meet, but cripes, give me a fair
crack of the whip! I've been readin' for a while now and
there's no gettin' around the big *C-O-N* and all those other
letters followed by an *XI*."

Vanderbilt laughed at the man's sarcastic wit, but
looked to Tate for confirmation of Nigel's assertion.
Understanding the question in his patron's eyes, the
museum curator responded with validation. "All the Roman
Caesars—at least those whose tombs we have found—were
laid on slabs of marble. Their names were always cut into the
stone. I'm curious, Mr. Bailey, was the marble of the rare,
dark variety? And the slab like a large gravestone?"

Nigel's eyes narrowed and he replied instantly. "I am
aware that I don't possess your sophistication, that to you I

am just some galah in kangaroo hide jumping around the
big city, but I don't appreciate being suspected of fraud."
Tate tried to interrupt but was stopped as Nigel held up a
hand. Softening, he said, "But seeing as how you have a job
to do"—Nigel looked at Vanderbilt—"and a fine one he is
doing . . ." Back to Tate, he continued. "I'll give you the
answers you need for verification. However," he warned with
a pointed finger, "no more mucking about with your sneaky
questions. I won't take kindly to it. I'm not in the mood."

Vanderbilt watched the exchange with interest. Tate had
paled at the Australian's aggressive posture. It was he who
had earlier suggested a series of traps to ensure the validity
of the material being offered for sale. Hoaxes were common, and he had already saved the museum from embarrassment on several occasions. Osborn, for his part,
maintained his composure and managed a stiff smile as he
grudgingly nodded.

Taking a deep breath, Nigel grinned and said, "Right. All
friends again? Here we go. No, the marble wasn't of the
'rare, dark variety.' It was pure white, as you well know. And
the great man wasn't lying on a slab like a gravestone. He
was lying on a slab like somebody's house! It was mam-
moth. I'd loved to have brought it along, but I didn't have
a herd of elephants with me at that moment to yank it out
of the ground. Criminy! Are they all that big?"

Tate tried to chuckle politely but was so nervous that his
laugh came out like a gargle. Nevertheless, he answered.
"Actually, yes, they are. The marble has always been white
and the blocks weighing in excess of thirty tons. It is a bit
of a mystery how they were placed to begin with.
Certainly, removing them has been ridiculously difficult.
Incidentally, I apologize for my obviously bumbled attempt

at subterfuge a moment ago. A person of Mr. Vanderbilt's position is often the target of those willing to take advantage of his generosity. I needed to have some assurance that you'd really found Constantine XI."

Changing the subject, Dr. Osborn asked, "Mr. Bailey, what do you know about Constantine?"

"A mite," Nigel answered with a shrug. "You don't rattle a man's bones and not become a speck curious about what was happening when they were walking about! In any event, I know you gents are on a schedule. So am I. You want it straight? Here's what I know: Emperor Constantine XI"—Nigel crossed his arms—"taken by the invading Turkish forces of Sultan Mehmet in 1453. Offered his life in exchange for the safety of his people, Constantine was rumored to have been slain by the sultan himself. His heroic death was legend, perhaps burnished a bit by the fact that no one knew where the bloke was buried. At least until yours truly hacked him out with a shovel.

"It was the mystery of a lifetime . . . buried in a secret location, giving rise to all manner of pious tales about 'the sleeping emperor,' in seclusion, one day to awaken, driving out the bloodthirsty barbarians and restoring the Holy Roman Empire. In conclusion: one, it's really him. Two, I've got some of his stuff. And three, I've seen the man. He's not sleepin'. He's bloody dead. My point being, he doesn't need the items anymore. They're worth a fortune and I'd like to sell them to you. There. That straight enough for you?"

Vanderbilt's eyes twinkled as he leaned forward. "Fine, Mr. Bailey. But you still haven't told me what you found inside the tomb."

Nigel kept a straight face. He had dreaded this question, for in truth, he had been unhappy with his haul. *All the dead kings in the world,* he thought, *and I have to find the tomb of the only poor one!* The carvings and pottery had a certain value, he knew, but there was nothing spectacular with which to fan the flame of a buyer's desire. Especially a buyer as cultured as the one before him.

"I have everything secreted away," Nigel replied calmly. Maintaining eye contact, he drew the medallion from his pocket and passed it to Vanderbilt. "But there's a sample. Keep it. I'm sure we can come to an arrangement on the rest."

"Possibly," the wealthy man said as he took the object. It was circular, flat, and about the size of his palm—plain and exquisite all at once. Vanderbilt was quite sure that the man before him was running a bit of a bluff. He was presenting this, the best of the lot, as a gift, and gambling that the remaining items would be purchased sight unseen. And indeed, Vanderbilt knew, he might do just that. *In this gentleman's mind,* Vanderbilt mused, *there is only merit in gold. He would never understand that I do not want or need another jewel. A centuries-old clay pot, now, I will spend some money on that!*

As Vanderbilt held the medallion up to catch the window's light, Nigel was glad he had taken the time to clean and polish it. While the disk had been reddish-brown and covered in dried organic matter, it was now a rich, gleaming bronze.

On one side of the medallion, carved letters wound around its outside edge. They were of a language with which Nigel was unfamiliar. In its center was an empty space about the size of a thumbnail, rough to the touch, as if something had once been there and was now broken off. On the other side of the disk, however, carved into its surface in a circular pattern, were dozens of the letters—symbols—tiny, but clearly defined. With a small stick and a rag,

Nigel had taken hours to clean the grooves of the script. The medallion was not gold, but it shined like the sun itself. "See the hole?" Nigel said. "Strap went through it. Man wore it around his neck."

Vanderbilt nodded, concentrating instead on the script. Tate leaned toward the medallion and, when he was noticed, reached out and said, "May I?"

Vanderbilt gave him the object and was alarmed as the expert held it into the light and immediately frowned. "What's wrong?" he asked.

Instead of answering, Tate nervously directed another question to Nigel. "You found *this* on the emperor?"

"That's right."

Tate looked at Nigel briefly as if to confirm that he had answered in the affirmative, then back to the medallion. His frown deepened.

"Lawrence, tell me," Vanderbilt said. "Is it bad news?"

Denyer, the valet, rose instantly, Nigel noticed, as if to be ready to protect his boss. *If he's trying to be subtle,* Nigel thought, *he's failing miserably.* "Have a seat, mate," he said aloud. "I'm not coming across the table." To Tate, he directed a question. "Let's be having it. Why the long face?"

Tate looked up, momentarily confused. He looked back and forth between Nigel and Vanderbilt as he spoke. "The piece is authentic. It's gorgeous. It's just that it doesn't fit the timeline history has established for Constantine. It's no problem actually—the emperors collected antiques just as we do."

They stared blankly at him. "What I mean is that Constantine died in 1453. This medallion is at least a thousand years older than that—maybe much older. And it's not Roman. It's Sumerian or . . . well, about that, I am not totally certain. Without a doubt, however, it *is* from that region of the world. The script is Akkadian or Aramaic. It just doesn't follow that a Roman emperor would be wearing . . . this."

"What did you say the script was?" Vanderbilt asked.

"Akkadian . . . Aramaic . . . I'm not prepared to make a determination at this juncture. They are both closely related and written in common symbolic arrangement. I can translate it, given some time. The larger letters on this side are . . . well, that is a symbol that means 'with' or 'by' and there are three symbols that spell or represent 'people.'" He paused. "Alfred, I know you are in a hurry . . ."

"Take your time," Vanderbilt said. "We have a few minutes. Can Ronald help?"

"Yes, actually. Ronald, take these notes for me, please. Before you leave, I'd like to understand this part, at least."

Tate huddled with the valet as the other three continued to talk and sip tea and coffee. "Business in Europe, Mr. Vanderbilt?" the Australian asked.

"Of a sort," he answered. "I'll be directing a meeting of the International Horse Breeders Association, but my main purpose in making the crossing is to offer a fleet of wagons to the Red Cross Society. I'll also offer myself as a driver. War is raging over there, as I am sure you are aware."

"Yeh. Certainly is in places. I barely made it out. Any farther north than Genoa, and all bets would've been off." Nigel couldn't help but ask a question of the statement Vanderbilt had hung in the air. "Not enough to give 'em the wagons? You're volunteering to drive them yourself?"

Vanderbilt gazed out the window for a moment and didn't answer. Then he said simply, "I don't feel as though I am doing enough."

"Excuse me," Dr. Tate said, bringing the attention back to the medallion and its translation. "I have several words finished on this side. Here you are. See this line of symbols that run the edge?" The men indicated that they did. "Here we have several word choices available. One scholar might translate this one way while another shifts a word or two.

"It makes little difference, however. Here is what I mean: I make it, '*With one's hand, safety is for all.*' It could also read, 'By one's hand,' or 'By your hand.' The second part also contains options. 'All are saved' or 'All will be saved.' 'The people' or 'the population' will or shall be saved . . ." Tate gestured with his hands as if to say "whatever."

Vanderbilt reached out and took the disk. "By one's hand, they will be saved?"

"It didn't do Constantine a lot of good," Nigel pointed out wryly.

Vanderbilt turned the object over and ran his fingers across the smooth surface. "According to the story," he said, "it was Constantine's hand that did the deed; it was the people who were saved."

Nigel, Osborn, Tate, and Denyer each contemplated that thought, patiently drinking their beverages while Vanderbilt studied the disk. "Any idea what's on the other side?" he said to Tate.

"There are well over a hundred symbols there. Each symbol might, by itself, represent a word or phrase. And there are more symbols I didn't complete on this side. I can do it, but it'll take some time. Leave it with me and I'll have it done by the time you return."

Vanderbilt seemed to ponder the offer briefly, then slipped the disk into his jacket pocket. "No, if you don't mind, I wish to carry it with me. 'With my hand' and all that . . . a bit of fire in my pocket perhaps—inspiration if you will—while I'm driving a Red Cross Wagon for the fighting men."

Momentarily the millionaire appeared to be deep in thought. Then, as if having made a decision, he said, "Lawrence, I'd like you to travel with me, if you don't mind. I want this translation as soon as possible. You can do it on the trip." Tate appeared startled, but catching Osborn's eye, agreed immediately.

"Ronald?" Vanderbilt continued. "Arrange passage for Dr. Tate when we reach port. First class, including his return. Since we'll be departing immediately and Dr. Tate is not prepared, make certain he has an unlimited account on board ship for clothes and essentials."

Vanderbilt turned to Nigel. "Mr. Bailey, at your leisure, sir, do drop by Dr. Osborn's office at the museum on Seventy-seventh. Please bring the remaining items from the tomb." He turned to the director. "Henry, you are hereby authorized to negotiate on my behalf and pay him from the fund we've established. Be fair with the man. I like him." Vanderbilt nodded at Nigel.

"Thank you, sir," Nigel said, shaking Vanderbilt's hand as they all stood.

The coach was waiting as Alfred Vanderbilt exited the pub. The driver held the door as he, then Dr. Tate, and at last Ronald stepped up into the finely appointed carriage and settled in for the trip to the port of New York. As the horses lurched forward, Alfred thought about the meeting that had just taken place. He shifted in the seat and removed the medallion from his pocket.

Seeing him examine the object, Ronald Denyer spoke. "It's beautiful, sir."

Vanderbilt nodded. "I think so too."

"Curious, though, wouldn't you say? The translation, the emperor, everything about it . . . just curious."

"Yes, it is," Vanderbilt agreed as he returned the object to his pocket. He was quiet for a time, watching the people on the sidewalks as the coach sped by. The rain had stopped altogether, he noticed. "Did you pack my evening shoes, Ronald?"

"Yes, sir."

"Good man. Have you familiarized yourself with the layout of the ship?"

"Yes, sir. And when we arrive, the Cunard representatives will meet us at the gangplank. I understand Captain Turner will welcome you personally."

"What suite did you reserve? Do you remember?"

"Yes, sir. I do. You are staying in the Regal. That's suite B-65 and 67. It is the best on board, sir."

"Thank you, Ronald," Vanderbilt acknowledged. "As usual, you have outdone yourself." Then, to Dr. Tate, he said, "We are in good hands with this man. You'll see, there will be nothing to worry about. Within a few minutes of our arrival, he'll have taken care of everything but an on-time departure." Then, turning back to Ronald, he teased, "Or have you seen to that, as well?"

The valet chuckled politely. "Not up to me, sir. But I shouldn't worry, if I were you. A schedule set in stone is a particular point of pride with Cunard. Yes, sir. The *Lusitania* is always on time."

⚜ Fourteen

New York City

SHE WAS A MIRACLE OF MODERN ENGINEERING, the largest of her breed. Docked at the Cunard line's Pier 54, the *Lusitania* was a portable skyscraper—her mastheads towered 216 feet into the air—blending easily with the New York City skyline. She stretched an astounding 785 feet, well beyond the Cunard docks and into the Hudson River, which had been dredged to accommodate her. A single walk around her promenade deck measured more than a quarter-mile.

Thousands of people crowded the docks, all to see the great ocean liner. Some managed to shake Vanderbilt's hand as he made his way amid the cheers and popping flashbulbs to the gangway. Striding up the incline ahead of his valet, Vanderbilt saw that the captain did indeed wait for him at the top.

"Bowler Bill" Turner was a commodore of the Cunard line. Fifty-nine years old, he was a large man with a close-cropped beard and white hair. Earlier that day, he had been

questioned as an expert witness in federal court. Judge Julius
Meyer presided over the legal proceedings that had been
convened to determine the financial liability of the White
Star Line in the sinking of the *Titanic*. Asked by the court
what lessons the shipping industry had learned from the disaster, Captain Turner, having solemnly sworn to tell the
whole truth, responded, "Nothing. And it will happen again."

Turner's appearance in court had made headlines in
every New York paper, and now, as he reached to shake the
captain's hand, Alfred Vanderbilt fleetingly thought of his
own narrow escape from that particular tragedy. In 1912,
two weeks before the ill-fated voyage, he had actually
reserved and paid for a suite on the *Titanic,* but had backed
out at the last minute.

"Welcome aboard, Mr. Vanderbilt, sir," Captain Turner
boomed as he grasped the millionaire's hand tightly. "It is an
honor to have you with us."

"Captain Turner, the honor is mine!" Vanderbilt coun-
tered humbly. "I consider it a privilege to be placed under
your command."

The captain laughed heartily. "I shall endeavor to keep
you from the dirtier work! I regret Mrs. Vanderbilt will not
be joining us."

"I shall miss her as well. As you may know, we have two
young sons. For their sake, she has chosen to stay in New
York and endure the squalor of our Park Avenue Hotel."

At that moment, as if on cue, a uniformed young man
stepped forward. "Steward," the captain addressed him,
"escort Mr. Vanderbilt to his suite."

"Aye, Captain," the steward said crisply. Quickly, he
relieved Denyer of a portion of his burden and led the way.
In a few short minutes, sixteen-year-old William Hughs

swung open the door for his charge. The Regal Suite, Vanderbilt admitted, certainly lived up to its name. One of two such staterooms on the ship, it contained two lavishly appointed master bedrooms, a private dining room, baths and toilets, all with ceilings burnished in gold. Marble fireplaces surrounded by oversized chairs were in each room. There was even a separate bedroom for Ronald, the valet.

After admiring the room, Vanderbilt left Ronald to take care of Dr. Tate and set out to explore the ship. He was pleased to meet an old friend, Charles Frohman, the impresario who had produced more than 500 theater productions on both sides of the Atlantic. Elbert Hubbard and his wife, Alice, Frohman informed him, were also passengers. Hubbard, the great American author, had sold 45 million copies of his most recent work, *A Message to Garcia.*

Making the turn and strolling the port side of the promenade deck, Vanderbilt stopped in the gift shop and, on impulse, purchased a jewelry box. It was of the finest-grade mahogany with a sliding grooved top. Its size was approximately four by six inches and the outside of the box had been covered in a fine, deep-purple fabric. *Beautiful,* he thought, *and a perfect resting place for the medallion.* Opening the box on the counter in the store, he removed the disk from his jacket pocket and placed it inside. Closing the top, he carefully carried the box back to his suite and put it on the shelf in his closet.

The sun finally burst through the clouds as the *Lusitania* got underway at 12:20 PM. With three earth-shattering blasts of her horn, the great ship gathered speed and sailed away. The crowds on the dock cheered, waved their handkerchiefs, and threw confetti as the ship's orchestra played "Tipparary" from one end of the boat deck while the Royal

Gwent Male Singers sang "The Star Spangled Banner" on the other.

Despite the knowledge that they were sailing into a European war zone, few of the passengers boarding had noticed that the ship's name and port of registry had been painted over in an effort to disguise her identity. Fewer still had seen the warning posted that morning in several New York newspapers. It was small—less than four inches high—and framed in black.

It read:

NOTICE!

Travelers intending to embark on the Atlantic voyage are reminded that a state of war exists between Germany and her allies and Great Britain and her allies; that the zone of war includes the waters adjacent to the British Isles; that in accordance with formal notice given by the Imperial German Government, vessels flying the flag of Great Britain, or any of her allies, are liable to destruction in those waters and that travelers sailing in the war zone on ships of Great Britain or her allies do so at their own risk.

IMPERIAL GERMAN EMBASSY
Washington, D.C.

Submarines in the vicinity of the British Isles had recently become a challenge for the Royal Admiralty. Prowling the English Channel and Irish Sea, the wolves of the ocean snapped at the heels of the stronger British Navy and had (more than a few times now) dealt crippling bites.

sailors. Ordering the U-20 to the surface, the commander rescued the animal and left the men to die. The dog later gave birth to a litter of puppies, every single one of which Schwieger kept on board the submarine.

Now Schwieger looked at the clock above the radio set. Soon, the U-20 would be clear of the Scottish coastline and free to surface and recharge her batteries. He kept watch through the periscope, anxious for that moment to arrive, as Gerta, a black-and-tan puppy and the only female from the litter, growled and tugged at his pants leg.

"There, there, Gerta," chuckled Raimund Weisbach, a young torpedo officer, "you are a ferocious hound and certain to replace the German shepherd as a dog of war, but do not harm my commander." Schwieger smiled at the comment, but never took his eyes from the periscope.

Charles Voegele, a nineteen-year-old electrician, was on the bridge as well. Conscripted from France the year before, Voegele was responsible for the care and feeding of the dachshunds in addition to his other duties. Despite his lack of status—after all, he was a Frenchman forced to fight for a country not his own—the young man was allowed unusual access to the captain's bridge because of the animals.

"Voegele," Schwieger directed, "take Gerta and secure the dogs." Then to Hermann Lanz, his pilot, he said, "In two minutes, take her up. Maintain course at fourteen knots. Set port and starboard watch." As an afterthought, he added, "Leave the hatch open and get some fresh air to the men."

As soon as he had given his orders, Schwieger exited the bridge and made his way to his berth. As commander, he was entitled to a curtain around the slim bunk—privacy was a submarine's greatest privilege—but the condensation that dripped from above and soaked the thin mattresses of

Most passengers, however, were not aware of the warning until the ship was on its way. Cunard and Captain Turner made every effort to downplay the notice and assure them that the *Lusitania,* at twenty-five knots, was much faster than any submarine could ever hope to be. "And besides," they scoffed, "the 'Lucy' is a cruise vessel. We have no military significance whatsoever! After all, there are only passengers onboard."

This, a blatant lie, wasn't to be uncovered for decades, but in truth, the *Lusitania* carried much more than human beings as cargo. A secret manifest revealed large amounts of aluminum to be used for bomb making, 50 cases of bronze powder, 1,250 cases of shrapnel shells, and 18 cases of fuses from the Bethlehem Steel Company. There were also 4,200 cases of Remington rifle cartridges, sorted 1,000 to a box, in the ship's holds as well. In truth, more than half the vessel's load was being shipped for the war effort, and as a U.S. Treasury official later lamented, "Practically all of her cargo was contraband of some kind." But then, food for the British people was also considered contraband by the Germans.

"You look splendid, sir," Ronald said as he straightened Vanderbilt's bow tie and fussed over the lint that always seemed to attach itself to the black tuxedo. It was almost 8 PM, and the millionaire was leaving the suite to meet Captain Turner and his other guests for dinner. "Dr. Tate is just down the hall in B-48 if you wish to see him. He's a bit ill, sir. The rocking of the ship, you know."

"Is this his first voyage?"

"I do believe that to be the case, sir. He intends to eschew dinner this evening in exchange for sleep and asked that he be permitted to begin his work in the morning."

"Of course," Vanderbilt responded. "I don't suppose there is any urgency . . . but I must admit to being overwhelmed with curiosity. Hat or no hat, Ronald?"

"No hat, sir," the valet replied. "You will be indoors all the way to the dining room. Do you wish me to escort you?"

"No, thank you," Vanderbilt said. "That won't be necessary. Though, on second thought, you might take my place at the table. It's certain to be quite stuffy."

Chuckling politely, the valet said, "There, there, out the door you go." Then, as an afterthought, he stopped and asked, "Sir? There is a purple jewel case on the shelf in your closet. Was it left by the steward?"

"No, no, Ronald," Vanderbilt said. "I apologize for not informing you. I purchased the box earlier from the ship's store. The medallion is in it."

"Ahh," the valet responded. "I didn't know. It is a beautiful case, sir."

"Yes," Vanderbilt agreed, "it is indeed. Leave it there, if you will, I want to look at the medallion again when I return."

"Might I examine it while you dine, sir?"

"Can't get it out of your mind either, is that it?" Vanderbilt grinned. "I understand the feeling. Certainly, Ronald. You know I don't mind. A unique piece, that. There is meaning attached, I'm sure of it. Call it a feeling if you will. And soon we will know what that meaning is!"

AT THAT VERY INSTANT, SEVEN MILES OFF THE northern shore of Scotland, Kapitänleutnant Walther von Schwieger swallowed hard in an effort to clear his ears. He had a dull, throbbing headache. *But then,* he thought, *I always have a headache.* The foul air—a mixture of sweat,

sewage, seawater, and oil fumes—were enough to driv man mad.

Schwieger had entered the German Imperial Nav the age of eighteen as a cadet and by the time he twenty-seven, captained his own U-boat. Now thirty, he commander of the U-20, en route to hunt the shore Liverpool. The U-20 was a diesel submarine that had commissioned in 1913—210 feet long and only 20 wide. Schwieger was proud of the boat and had bee skilled in the use of her optics, instruments, and torpe

A tall, handsome man, Schwieger had short blon and sharp facial features. He was commanding a full for this voyage—four officers and thirty-one seame of whom loved and feared him. He had proven his to keep them out of danger, but privately, each man veled at his ruthlessness. In January of that year, coast of France, he had torpedoed a merchant ship. V while she sank, he watched the drowning crew thro submarine's periscope and subsequently sank two merchant ships as they arrived to attempt a rescue.

In February, without giving warning, Schwieger torpedo at the British hospital ship *Asturias*. He because of torpedo failure, but later defended his a insisting that the ship had been an enemy troo port—a stunning assertion in view of the fact *Asturias* was painted white—with red crosses on more than thirty feet high.

Schwieger was an enigma to his crew. His thir enemy verged on barbarism, yet at times, he hearted to the point of recklessness. Once, after Portuguese schooner, he spotted a dachshund th periscope. The dog was swimming among the

the lowliest seaman, plagued him as well. Nevertheless, as Schwieger lay down for the first time since leaving Emden, the German Naval base, more than thirty-six hours earlier, he was asleep before the wet bed soaked through his uniform to his skin.

THE UNUSUALLY CALM SEAS HAD MANAGED TO brighten everyone's mood as the *Lusitania* made her way across the ocean. The current of nervous tension running through the passengers, which had been so apparent on the day of departure, quickly gave way to the luxurious routine of eating, being entertained, drinking, and eating again. Six days had now passed rather quickly.

Dr. Tate's seasickness had passed quickly as well and never returned. The first full day at sea, he had decided to finish the translation of the portion of the medallion on which he had already begun. By noon, he had settled on the wording, *By your hand, the people shall be saved.*

By the end of the third day, the translation had been completed. To Tate, the disk's contents seemed to be a communication of sorts and a strangely personal one, at that. Though he never mentioned it to Vanderbilt, the shy museum curator couldn't shake the odd feeling that the medallion's message was directed to him.

Vanderbilt was struck with the same thought. The medallion moved him somehow in a way he could not describe. As he read the translation for the first time, he had been shocked and embarrassed to burst into tears in front of Dr. Tate and Ronald, his valet. Yet he continued to weep as he read the words over and over, holding the disk in his hand. Never had he felt such a sense of purpose . . . and of value.

Vanderbilt spent days four, five, and six at sea contemplating the medallion's message. Ronald and Tate were no less intrigued. Their questions were without end. Who wrote the words? For whom were they intended? When were they composed? Why?

Vanderbilt had also, quite uncharacteristically, taken a great deal of time to himself. Of course, to a celebrity of consequence, especially a friendly one, any degree of privacy requires that one simply remain in one's suite.

He was happy to do just that and utilized the solitude to simply close his eyes and think. He was intrigued to find his mind refusing to focus on his usual passions, such as horses or art—even the mission of mercy he was undertaking for the Red Cross Society seemed strangely abstract and far away. His children, however, were unceasingly present in his thoughts—their faces and voices flitting in and out of his musing like tiny birds determined to land on his shoulder. It was unsettling, as if there was an itch that could not be scratched or something he could not remember.

Several times during these moments, he took the jewel case from the closet shelf and opened it, holding the disk in his hands, tracing the symbols with his fingertips and feeling a sense of certainty wash over him. Once, he even laid down on the bed and placed the medallion on his chest, but, feeling foolish, and not wishing to be seen in that position should Ronald enter the room, he quickly placed the disk back into the box and the box back into the closet.

It disconcerted him somewhat that he had become so reflective. It was unlike him, he knew. Yet for some reason, during this entire voyage, his thoughts had consistently returned to questions about his legacy, his responsibility, and his example. *What will my boys become?* he asked himself. *Will they be like me? And if they do, is that a good thing? What have I become? I have been given so much. What have I given in return? What really matters?*

At this moment, Alfred Vanderbilt stood alone in the cool afternoon, leaning against the port railing near the Verandah Café with its beautiful wicker chairs and tables. He could hear the sliding sounds of shuffleboard and the shouts of the winners from the deck above him. There seemed to be an unusual number of children onboard, Vanderbilt thought idly as his mind drifted again to his boys back in New York. *They would love to see this.* He had been watching flying fish, disturbed by the passing of the ship, leap into the air and travel hundreds of feet before finally splashing down again into the water.

"A penny for your thoughts, Alfred," a voice interrupted, breaking the calm that Vanderbilt had been enjoying. "Or do your thoughts require a higher bid?" It was Charles Frohman, the impresario. He approached with the aid of an oddly shaped wooden walking stick that he had lately begun calling "his wife." Unmarried and in considerable pain from the rheumatism in his hip, the cane was his only constant companion.

Vanderbilt laughed politely. "Hello, C. F."

Frohman stopped and rested, his back against the rail. Short and more than a bit overweight, he had been described as "a frog" in print by several newspaper critics jealous of his wealth and power, but he was well liked and could count Vanderbilt among his friends. "If they come for us," Frohman said with a teasing grin, "it will be tonight."

Vanderbilt responded with a smile. "Are you giving odds yet on when the kaiser will invade Washington?"

Frohman snorted a laugh. Pausing to light a cigar, he

said, "Seriously, were you aware that the captain has ordered the crew to black out all windows and portholes for this evening?"

Vanderbilt continued to look out over the sea, but his expression darkened. "No, I hadn't heard that."

"It's true. I've just now come by your suite on Promenade. I have the other Regal, you know, on the port side. In any case, your steward—the boy—was fastening black drapes to your windows. They are also closing the watertight doors. Say, will you be attending the talent show tonight?"

"Yes," Vanderbilt said simply. Then, back to the subject of possible danger, he wondered aloud. "I suppose you're right. Tonight would be the night. We'll practically be on shore tomorrow, isn't that correct?"

Frohman nodded. "We'll see the coast of Ireland before noon—that's what I'm told—and from that point we literally hug the coastline for the rest of the voyage. Then, it's a quick duck into the channel and a sprint to Liverpool. She'll be docked by eight o'clock tomorrow evening. Do you know how to put on your life jacket?"

Vanderbilt turned with an exasperated smile to look his friend directly in the face. With his eyes opened wide, he said, "C. F., my, but aren't you the bucket of cheer! Wouldn't you prefer to stalk the deck above? Maybe give the children playing shuffleboard a good scare?"

The shorter man shrugged self-consciously. "I don't mean to be . . . well, I'm sorry. It's on my mind. Some of the passengers have formed a committee. They are teaching as many as will listen how to properly fasten a life jacket. Staff Captain Anderson scolded them for causing unnecessary fear."

"There are signs all over the ship about the life jackets."

"No one has read them." Frohman puffed his cigar and watched Vanderbilt from the corner of his eye. "Have *you* read them?"

The millionaire didn't answer. Instead, he asked, "What is your estimate of our present speed?"

"Slow! 'Slow' is my estimate," Frohman barked. "We are six days at sea. You, yourself, know that the *Lusitania* once made the voyage from New York to Liverpool in five days—six, many times—and yet here we are . . . paddling along at eighteen knots. Why, when she can do twenty-six?"

"It has been foggy almost every night, C. F."

"Well, it's not foggy now," Frohman practically yelled.

Conceding the point, Vanderbilt raised another possibility. "Perhaps Captain Turner is intending to increase his speed this evening. And remember, British warships are patrolling these waters as well. I've been assured we will receive multiple naval escorts into the channel."

Frohman tossed his unfinished cigar into the water far below and sighed. "One last comment, Alfred, then I promise to leave the subject for good, and we can join the talent show. Here it is: I have listened carefully to the condescending drivel heaped upon us by Captain Turner and his ilk, and I must tell you, old son, their words of 'safety' ring hollow to me. I have been in the entertainment business all my life and have seen more convincing acting jobs from dance-hall girls.

"I am quite certain that it does not even slightly matter whether we have an escort, multiple escorts, or no escort at all! These deep-water, daughters of the devil are depressingly unfair. One cannot defend against that which one cannot see. These submarines are cowardly assassins, sneaking up behind a man and blowing his brains out. They are new weapons for a world that has changed, my friend . . . and no one asked my opinion before they made the changes."

THE MEN FOUND THE FIRST-CLASS SALOON FILLED to overflowing. This was not only one of the more popular events of the voyage, but an opportunity for the second-class passengers to enter what was an otherwise off-limits area.

It was almost 11 PM when the last performer—an elderly man pounding out a barely recognizable Irving Berlin tune on the piano—finally finished. Though the passenger talent show was a tradition on all ocean liners and usually enjoyed by everyone, this particular production held little interest for Captain Turner. His only purpose in attending at all had been to make an effort at calming the restless passengers and perhaps quelling some of the rumors that were becoming rampant. Anxious to return to the bridge, the captain nevertheless put a smile on his face and, applauding dutifully for the dreadful keyboard mauling he had just witnessed, stepped up onto the stage.

"As many years as I have been at sea," he said, as the room hushed, "I can honestly say that this particular passenger list, for whatever reason, holds the finest display of pure, unmitigated talent I have ever seen . . . and it was all on this stage this evening!" The audience applauded again as the captain joined them, nodding his head vigorously in agreement. "I should also like to take this opportunity to assure everyone of your absolute safety . . ."

Charles Frohman, seated at a table with Vanderbilt leaned over to him and whispered loudly, "Unbelievable! The man has been onstage for two seconds. He's covered two subjects with two sentences—and already told two lies!"

If the captain heard him, he gave no indication. Vanderbilt, on the other hand, struggled mightily to refrain from bursting out with laughter. "Be quiet, C. F.!" he ordered in an amused, but considerably softer, voice. "You have an admirable immunity to embarrassment, but the rest of us haven't been vaccinated!"

Frohman beamed with pleasure at the remark. His life in the theater had imbued him with a great appreciation for witty repartee, and Vanderbilt could always be counted upon to display his mastery.

"On entering the war zone tomorrow," Captain Turner was saying, "we shall be securely in the care of the Royal Navy. Of course there is no need for alarm. Please enjoy the rest of your evening, and in closing, may I remind the gentlemen, due to the blackout conditions, please avoid lighting any tobacco on deck. Smoking indoors only. Thank you, and good night."

As the audience stood to applaud the captain's exit, Frohman opened his mouth to speak. Before he could utter a word, Vanderbilt interrupted. "I know, C. F. I heard him. 'You are absolutely safe, but for goodness' sake, don't light a match and let them see us.' Yes, I heard it too." Frohman smiled, nodding, then suddenly frowned, deciding it wasn't that funny after all.

THE COMMANDER SAT IN THE ONLY CHAIR ON THE bridge with Gerta asleep in his lap. Except for Lanz, who was monitoring the controls, and Voegele, who stood at attention just outside the room, most of the men were sleeping. The U-20 was ballasted perfectly for seventy feet and drifting with the currents. Schwieger spit onto the

sub's floor, drank from a canteen of oily water, and spit on
the floor again. He could not rid his mouth of its metallic
taste—or his mind, the thought of it.

The curved walls of the tiny space reflected unearthly
shadows as the green glow of the instrument panel bored
through Schwieger's eyes and deeply into his brain, com-
pounding his ever-present headache. He hated nights like
this—the total waste of time! Darkness, by itself, had never
been a problem. Schwieger could always depend upon a
quickly opened door or the cigarette of a disobedient
crew member to yield just enough light for betrayal.
Darkness with fog, however, was a different story.

The year before, Schwieger had almost been rammed by
a ship he had not seen until the last moment. Cruising on
the surface, recharging the wet-cell batteries, he had narrowly
averted disaster when a freighter appeared out of the fog less
than a hundred feet away. He dived under its bow, actually
scraping the tail fin of the U-20, but was so shaken by the
experience that he never thought to turn and torpedo the
ship that had almost sunk him. Ever since that night, when
fog rolled in, Schwieger dived the U-20 to safe levels, well
underneath the spinning propellers of other vessels that, at
close range, were as dangerous to him, as he was to them.

On the morning of May 7, the commander ordered the
submarine to the surface at five o'clock, six o'clock, and
then again at seven to find the same motionless fog that
had plagued the U-20 all night. Schwieger continued to
monitor the conditions every hour until, at ten o'clock, the
curtain of smoky mist had sufficiently lifted, allowing the
day's hunt to begin. At that moment, records reveal that
Commander Schwieger's U-20 and Captain Turner's
Lusitania were eighty-five miles apart.

⚹ Fifteen

DAYLIGHT CAME AS A WELCOME RELIEF FOR THE passengers and crew of the great ocean liner. As the morning wore on and the thick fog burned off, people gathered on deck, greeting each other, increasingly comfortable in the knowledge that the voyage was almost over. At 11:45, the western tip of Ireland was sighted off the port bow, causing great cheers and congratulations among passengers and crew alike.

Five minutes later, in the U-20, Commander Schwieger ordered Lanz to dive. His lookouts had reported a navy cruiser steaming directly toward them. Unsure as to whether he had actually been spotted, Schwieger drifted the sub quietly at seventy-nine feet until they plainly heard the diesels of the British warship *Juno* passing directly overhead. He ascended warily to thirty-six feet in hopes of launching a torpedo, but watched through the periscope as the *Juno,* thwarting any attempt on her life, zigzagged, changing course and speed, all the way into Queenstown.

Schwieger decided to remain in the area, patrolling the harbor mouth for at least the day, watching, waiting for another ship to make its way into the Irish port. Or for one to try to come out.

The *Lusitania* edged ever closer to the incredible green of the coastline. It seemed that the entire ship's population was on deck enjoying the increasing view of land after so long at sea. Chief Purser McCubbin had his binoculars out and was sharing them with anyone who wanted to look. A newspaper photographer was busy making extra money by taking pictures of anyone who wanted a memento of the trip.

When the U-20 surfaced at 1:20 PM, Charles Voegele noticed the calm seas immediately and, though not allowed topside as the hatch was opened, he inhaled the fresh air and breathed a silent prayer of thanks. Seasickness tormented the young man, and as might have been expected, he received no sympathy from the crew. *But I am not a sailor!* he wanted to scream. Taken from his family's farm by force, Voegele was compelled by threat of death—his family's as well as his own—to serve the Imperial German Navy in whatever capacity they might deem appropriate.

Voegele's skills as an electrician eventually landed him aboard the U-20 where by his own reckoning, he had been vomiting, about to vomit, or just finished vomiting, ever since. *Life is very good,* he thought, displaying to himself the sense of humor that he had not lost and that, in fact, had kept him sane. *I am standing at attention just outside the bridge of a tin cigar that is commanded by a psychopath who slaughters people and kisses dogs!*

Suddenly, Voegele became aware of a commotion in the control room as Weisbach, the torpedo officer who had been on watch, slid down the ladder, excitedly jabbering to Schwieger about "many ships" and "a forest of masts and stacks." The young French conscript did not catch every word, but understood enough German to realize that the sub was being readied for an attack.

"Tauchen!" Schwieger ordered. "Alarm! Everyone to diving stations!"

Moments later, as the U-20 blew her ballast tanks and canted downward, the commander deployed the periscope. "Lanz—level at thirty-six feet. Weisbach—where are the ships?"

"On the horizon, sir. Port, twenty degrees."

For several stressful moments, the men quietly waited for their commander's next words. Finally, Schwieger lifted his head from the periscope and ordered, "Maintain course. Full speed. Weisbach, there are not multiple targets. The masts and stacks you saw are from one ship. She is less than four miles away. I want everyone at battle stations."

As the submarine crew prepared the U-20 for action, Schwieger reset the periscope and watched the ship carefully. She was steering an uneven course, though her speed seemed constant. Soon the target was less than three miles away.

"Engineering is ready, sir," a man reported as he appeared at the entrance to the control room.

"Fine," Schwieger said as he backed away from the metal column of the periscope. "Here . . . take a look. Sturmer, isn't it?"

"Yes, sir. Thank you, sir," the engineer acknowledged as he settled his face into the periscope sight. Schwieger had long practiced the leadership principle of involving all subordinates. He encouraged every member of the U-20 crew—from the officers to the conscripts—to occasionally take a turn viewing targets through the periscope. In any case, the long approaches before an attack were usually more waiting than anything else. Rather than mindlessly performing a duty day after day with no idea where one's efforts fit into the scheme of things, Schwieger felt that a few moments now and again in the very position of authority kept them involved and gave them a sense of the team's mission. It was good for morale.

"An excellent target, sir," Sturmer said as he stepped away. "Thank you for the opportunity."

"Thank you for your work, Sturmer," the commander replied as he looked again through the periscope and checked the target's progress. Quickly, he allowed two other men to take their turns seeing the ship as it steamed closer. Then, repositioning himself in front of the faceplate, Schwieger readied himself for the final run.

"She is two miles and closing," he said. All was quiet for several minutes until Schwieger ordered, "Come starboard . . . five degrees. Eight degrees. Starboard, eight degrees!" he said louder. "Ahh . . . no. No, no!" Schwieger cursed. "Ach! She is changing course!" He watched a moment, then cursed again. Pushing himself away from the eyepiece and slapping at the periscope as if it had let him down, the commander told his officers, "A massive target—30,000 tons, at least— and we are out of position! There is nothing we can do."

It was true. The *Lusitania* was steaming a route that would place her well beyond the reach of the U-20. By altering her course, the liner had become the apparent victor of this winner-take-all game of blindman's buff. The contest was played out twenty-four hours a day in these waters, and the stakes were life itself.

This was a game in which the submarines held all the

cards. Like a bully in one's backyard, the sub commanders
made up the rules as they went along . . . and everyone else
was forced to play their way. The guidelines were simple:
*My ship can do only one-third the speed of your ship. But you
don't know where I am. Proper positioning wins all contests . . .
and you will never know where that proper position is. As you race
into an area, I will have maneuvered there ahead of you. Your
speed merely brings you to my fist.*

In the dark Atlantic waters of 1915, submarines had the
home-team advantage. They competed with the fearless-
ness of an undefeated champion. In gambling parlance,
they were "the house."

In all games of chance, the odds favor the house. One
may enter the game with high ideals, a feeling of invinci-
bility, a system for success, or an optimistic attitude. One
may even do well for a time . . . but old adages are seldom
proven wrong. And it is dangerous to forget that when the
stakes are your life and the game is played for keeps—
sooner or later the house always wins.

Such was the probability when the *Lusitania* changed
course again. As Schwieger watched in wonder through
the periscope, the pride of Britain steadily turned and
made directly for the U-20. Schwieger later recorded in his
war diary: *She could not have steered a more perfect course if she
had deliberately tried to give us a dead shot. A short fast run and
we waited.*

The rudder of the submarine kept her in place despite
the strong current. The U-20 hung at exactly thirty-six feet
as Commander Schwieger tersely called out coordinates.
"Range is four thousand feet and closing to our starboard.
Estimated speed of target . . . seventeen knots. Weisbach?"
The answer was not quick enough. "Weisbach!"

"Yes, Commander!"

"Arm the torpedo. Set depth to ten feet."

"Yes, sir."

Schwieger, sensing a person close by, looked away from the periscope for a second and saw Charles Voegele standing there with Gerta under his arm. In actuality, he had just captured the dog as she was about to run between the commander's legs. Schwieger, however, misunderstood the boy's presence and assuming he wanted to look through the periscope, spoke sharply. "This is not the time, Voegele! Quickly, look." The boy started to explain, but Schwieger snapped fiercely, "Do it! Do it now!" So, he did.

The commander turned to double-check Weisbach's work, touching and mentally listing the settings on the torpedo hydroplanes and rudder. "Lanz!" he called. "Speed?"

"Current drift, three knots, sir. Holding steady."

"Excellent," Schwieger said as he stepped back to the periscope. Gerta, on the floor for some reason, jumped against his leg. He clenched his jaw and ignored the distraction of the puppy, which was now running free in the control room. She barked once, then again, as the commander said, "Voegele, get the dog."

"*Nein*," the young electrician answered.

No was a word not often heard on a German submarine, and it was doubtful whether Commander Schwieger had *ever* heard it. The word, spoken aloud, produces a simple sound, short and easily duplicated, but with a power all its own. Everyone heard it. And despite the tension and immediacy of the moment, everyone stopped what they were doing and stared at Voegele. He still gripped the handles of the periscope though he was no longer looking into the viewfinder. The blood had drained from his face.

"What did you say?" Schwieger asked in stunned disbelief. Then, realizing he had but moments to act and knowing he would be able to deal with the incident later, he didn't wait for an answer. Instead, he ordered, "Move, Voegele," and received the same response.

"*Nein.*"

This time, there was no hesitation. With the back of his hand, Commander Schwieger hit the boy across the face, tearing him loose from the periscope and sending him flying into the wall of the control room, where he slid to the floor. Grasping the handles and pulling the periscope into place, Schwieger found the target in the eyepiece and said, "Range is twenty-four hundred feet. Speed is still—"

"It is a passenger vessel!" Charles Voegele croaked from where he had landed. "There are women and children aboard. I saw them."

Lanz and Weisbach, confused, looked from their commander to the electrician, who was now bleeding from the nose, and back to Schwieger, who called out, "Twenty-one hundred. Prepare to fire."

"We cannot do this!" Voegele screamed as he struggled to his feet. "I saw a baby. There are mothers with babies on that ship!"

"Sir?" It was Weisbach, the torpedo officer. He said the word with the barest question in his voice.

In one continuous, fluid motion, Schwieger pointed at Weisbach, hissing, "I said, 'Prepare to fire,'" and then grabbed Voegele by the shirt front and savagely ran his head into the steel wall. Dropping him unconscious to the floor, the commander gripped the periscope yet again.

"Range, eighteen hundred. *Los!*" Shoot! A tremor ran through the U-20 as the torpedo left the bow tube.

"Torpedo away," Weisbach reported.

"Time, Lanz. Log the time, please," Schwieger requested.

"2:09, sir."

ALFRED VANDERBILT WAS SEATED WITH CHARLES Frohman and Staff Captain Anderson by a window on the starboard side of the first-class dining room. Having finished their meal, the three were joined by Elbert Hubbard, who had eaten with his wife, Alice, at another table. She had retired to their suite for a nap, leaving the men to enjoy the afternoon together—a last hurrah before they arrived in Liverpool that evening.

The orchestra in the front of the dining room was playing "The Blue Danube Waltz." As they talked and drank coffee, Vanderbilt was amused to notice a boy at the next table—seven or eight years old—who had become fascinated by a tiny spot of reflected sunlight that was bouncing around his table and the column next to it. Alfred quickly realized that the reflection was a product of the sun beaming through the window and catching the cuff link of his left sleeve. It produced a bright, pinpoint reflection that Vanderbilt was able to control by tilting his wrist slightly this way or that.

The boy, who reminded the millionaire so much of his older son, was mesmerized by the dancing dot of light. When at last he figured out what was happening and who was teasing him, the boy broke into a broad grin. Vanderbilt laughed out loud.

"What's so funny, Alfred?" Hubbard asked, seeing the boy laugh as well.

"The sunlight caught my cuff link. I was teasing the boy

by . . ." Vanderbilt frowned. Mentioning the sun, he had glanced over his left shoulder, giving his peripheral vision a split second to register a disturbance on the smooth water in the distance. He turned in his seat and held a hand to his brow, shading his eyes, trying to find the object that had captured his attention a moment earlier.

"What is it, sir?" the staff captain asked.

"I don't know. I saw something . . . there!" Another man, two tables beyond them, but also next to the window was standing, pointing out the same object to the people at his table. Moving steadily, it was three hundred yards or so away—too far to see clearly or identify.

All four men were standing. "Is it a dolphin?" Frohman asked. No one answered. "Is it a dolphin?" he asked a second time.

"Is that . . . whatever it is . . . is it paralleling us?" Hubbard asked Vanderbilt. "Or is it . . . you know . . ." Then to Anderson, "Do you see it?" The staff captain nodded.

Everyone in the dining room stood now. The orchestra had stopped in the middle of their performance and was crowding the starboard windows with everyone else. The object was about 150 yards away when Staff Captain Anderson suddenly gasped, "Dear God!" and wheeled away.

At the same instant, a woman shrieked the word *Torpedo!* and as if someone had flipped a switch, the place was bedlam. Screams and curses filled the air as people pushed and punched, desperate to exit the dining room.

Calmly, as if watching the story line of a great Broadway drama unfold, Vanderbilt leaned his forehead against the glass. The torpedo was moving in a swift, straight line, throwing a white wake as it bubbled along the surface, now only fifty yards away.

From where he stood inside the dining room, Alfred was unable to watch the final few yards of the torpedo's track. It appeared to him as though the missile had simply disappeared under the ship. He had actually considered this possibility—the moment of impact—several times during the past six days. In his mind's eye, Vanderbilt had always conjured a scene reminiscent of the *Titanic,* which had involved a relatively silent ripping of the ship's hull.

Newspaper accounts of that tragedy revealed that most passengers had actually needed to be informed that they were sinking. To most of them, the physical evidences of danger were almost undetectable for nearly an hour, and as word had spread through the ship, people took time to pack, to write letters, or to listen to the orchestra, which had continued to play. In total, it seemed to Vanderbilt that the *Titanic* disaster had been, everything considered, a rather orderly affair. After all, she had taken more than four hours to sink. Even had Vanderbilt somehow gained foreknowledge of the events that were about to play out, it would still have been inconceivable to him that the *Lusitania* would sink in less than eighteen minutes.

When the torpedo found its mark, it did so between the second and third funnels—slightly ahead of the *Lusitania*'s dead center. Michael Byrne, an accountant from Philadelphia, described the impact as "a million-ton hammer hitting a steel boiler." The subsequent explosion threw water, wood, and hot steel a hundred feet in the air. But a mysterious *second* explosion, following the first in the blink of an eye, actually lifted the bow of the ship out of the water.

Debris showered the decks, injuring many of the panic-stricken passengers, most of whom had been enjoying the sunshine and blue skies of the last afternoon of their cruise. For most of them, it would be the last afternoon of their lives.

Captain Turner ordered the lifeboats lowered to the promenade deck. "Make certain that the women and children get aboard first," he instructed.

Bob Leith, the wireless operator, had begun transmitting an SOS with their location, but knew that the electricity was failing. He had hopes, however, for the emergency generators. His assistant had fled his post as soon as the explosion occurred.

Making his way along the promenade deck, Vanderbilt was intending to go to his suite. When the torpedo had struck, his first thought had been of his family and the favorite photograph of his boys that was on his bedside table. Having traveled with it for years, he was determined to save that, at least. The medallion on the shelf in his closet was also on his mind.

Vanderbilt saw Frohman standing by the rail, out of the way of the stampeding people. Dodging across the deck, Alfred reached his older friend. "Are you all right, C. F.?" Vanderbilt asked.

"Yes, thank you, Alfred." Frohman had the barest hint of a smile. "What would you say the list is at present? Ten degrees? Fifteen?"

"Fifteen, C. F., and she's tilting more by the second. Come with me. We need to get the life jacket from your suite. I *did* read the instructions after your little speech yesterday. Hurry now."

"No, my boy," Frohman smiled, "I shall be fine right here. Thank you though. After all, 'why fear death? It is the most beautiful adventure that life gives us.'" Seeing the odd look on his friend's face, the theatrical producer added,

"Peter Pan!" as if Vanderbilt should have recognized the quote.

At 2:14, the electricity, including all generators, failed completely, plunging the interior of the ship into total darkness. The steel-caged elevators stopped as well, most between floors and packed with screaming passengers who could not see or escape. Only four minutes had passed since the torpedo had detonated, but the catastrophe was well underway.

Many of the men trapped in crew elevators had been specifically trained in the operation of the complicated lowering of the lifeboats. Their inability to free themselves ensured the deaths of many, in addition to their own.

As Vanderbilt left Charles Frohman, he saw men attempting to board a lifeboat and being held away by a crew member with an ax. "Not yet!" the sailor screamed. "Not yet!"

Alfred sidestepped neatly to avoid the terror-stricken mob of running people and ducked into the dark hallway near his suite. He ran squarely into Dr. Tate and Ronald, his valet, who were being pushed from behind by the steward, young William Hughs. Each of them held an armload of life jackets.

Quickly, they helped one another into the jackets and tied them tightly. "I need to get to the suite," Vanderbilt said.

"I'm sorry, sir," Ronald replied. "The explosions were on this side and must have damaged the balance of the walls. The doors are jammed."

"We even took an ax to them," Hughs added. "No use."

"I insisted we try the ax, sir," Ronald said. "I knew you would want the photograph of the boys." Giving his boss a knowing look, the valet added, "And I thought you might want the purple box."

Vanderbilt blinked, then said softly, "Very well, then." Taking some life jackets into his own arms, he turned and led them out into the chaos of the deck.

By 2:17, Chief Purser McCubbin was beginning to ignore the danger in which the ship's condition placed them all. He had become more concerned with the immediate safety of several of the *Lusitania's* more prominent passengers—for he thought he might kill them himself! More than a dozen people crowded around him, demanding that he proceed without delay to his office—where the ship's safe was located—and retrieve their valuables. Speaking to a woman who wore a life jacket over her fur coat, McCubbin said, "Madam! If we make port, you may claim your jewelry at that time. If we do *not* make port, it won't really matter that much, will it?"

About half the people Vanderbilt passed had their life jackets on incorrectly. With their heads through armholes or backwards and upside down, passengers seemed incapable of properly fastening a life jacket, and many, unable to get to their cabins, did not have the jackets at all. Fights broke out among some of the more desperate. One officer, having told a woman, "Get your own life jacket! It's every man for himself," was beaten badly by her husband, who took the man at his word . . . and took the officer's life jacket as well.

Vanderbilt, Ronald, Tate, and William had begun to help with life jackets when the first of several rumors inexplicably swept the *Lusitania* at 2:18. "The ship has been saved!" people reassured each other. "Pumps are now discharging the water she has taken on and soon the electricity will be restored." Passengers and crew alike actually stopped, straightened, and began to smile and shake hands, congratulating themselves and laughing nervously about the stories they would have to tell when they got home. But Vanderbilt looked to the front of the ship and, seeing her bow almost underwater, knew it was not true. Within the space of seconds, so did everyone else, and the pandemonium that had been oddly halted by a brief, civil interlude, continued. Calmly, Alfred picked up another life jacket and looked for someone on whom to place it.

During that brief period of false hope, many of the passengers saw the periscope of the U-20. Schwieger had moved close to the ship, intending to observe her final moments. He recorded in his diary: *Clean bow shot. Torpedo hit starboard side right behind the bridge. An unusually strong explosion took place.*

As Schwieger maneuvered around the stricken ship, Voegele regained consciousness and left the control room. He was later court-martialed for his actions that day and spent three years in prison for his offense.

Meanwhile, on board the *Lusitania,* the lifeboats were filled to overflowing or totally empty, depending upon their location. With the vessel listing hard to starboard, the port side lifeboats swung into the ship, practically resting on the promenade deck itself. The starboard boats, however, swung away from the ship, exposing a gap of almost six feet between the promenade railing and the boats. In effect, though there was a sufficient number of lifeboats on board, a large number of them on the port side could not be lowered, while on the starboard, they could not be reached.

It was approximately 2:20 when the ship momentarily leveled, allowing the first lifeboat to be lowered. It was so overloaded that the crew manning the ropes on one end released their hold faster than intended, outdistancing the crew on the other end. The lifeboat, aiming for a controlled, horizontal descent, now hung by one end, vertically, spilling its passengers into the water from forty feet in the air. Other crews, hurrying to lower boats while they could, made mistakes that bound boats permanently to the ship with tangled lines or crashed them into splinters against its side.

The crew and passengers, in some cases, were also pitted against each other. One seaman, struggling to steady a wildly swinging lifeboat, suddenly found a pistol pointed to his head, wielded by a man who demanded that he "let go the rope and help him in the boat!" The sailor tried to explain that, with the help of a block and tackle, his rope was the only thing holding the lifeboat off the deck and away from the tilting wall of the promenade deck. The crazed passenger would hear no excuse. He cocked the handgun and, threatening to shoot, howled at the crewman, "Let go the rope!" So the crewman did, and quickly jumped out of the way as the lifeboat, weighing almost seven thousand pounds, crashed down to the deck, into the wall, and directly on top of the man with the gun.

Lifeboats on the port side, one after another, dumped their passengers into the cold ocean below. Many, despite their life jackets, were already dying. The fifty-two-degree water added to the shock and quickly numbed extremities, making it difficult to escape pieces of the *Lusitania* herself that had begun detaching and raining down on those who were fortunate enough (or unfortunate enough) to still be floating. It was later determined that of all the port side lifeboats, only one had been successfully launched and gotten safely away from the ship.

On the starboard side, after the perfect launch of a boat filled with women and children, crew members watched in horror as another lifeboat, fully loaded, came loose from its ropes and fell unencumbered, landing squarely on top of the first, crushing most of the people in it and scattering the rest to the sea.

Baby buggies, often with children inside, careened wildly around the tilting deck. Many of the mothers, after determining their inability to make the leap from ship to lifeboat, began throwing their babies across the gap. Some were successful; others were not. In any case, dozens of women began pushing their children into the hands of total strangers, hoping that *anyone* else might be better equipped to protect the child.

Charlotte Pye, the young wife of a doctor from Connecticut, had been separated from her husband. Running from lifeboat to lifeboat with her three-year-old, Marjorie, she was repeatedly denied boarding. "Full! We are full!" the terrified passengers would cry as they approached. Continually knocked off her feet by the advancing list of the mortally wounded ship, she never let go of her daughter, though by the number of children she noticed wandering the decks alone, it was evident that many others had already done so.

Thrown to the deck again, Charlotte felt herself being hauled up by the arm. She recognized the man who helped her to a sheltered alcove as the millionaire, Alfred Vanderbilt. "Don't cry," he said. "It's quite all right."

"No, it isn't," she sobbed. "We have no life jackets, I don't know where my husband is, and this ship is going to sink."

"I believe you are correct, madam, and it won't be long now, by the looks of things." He called for Ronald, who was helping an elderly couple with their life jackets. Finishing that task, he ran to Vanderbilt immediately.

"Any more life jackets?" he asked the valet, who shook his

head no, causing Charlotte to begin crying again. "There, now,"Vanderbilt said, as he untied his own life jacket,"didn't I tell you everything would be all right?" He tied the mother and her baby into the jacket and pointed them toward a higher deck.

As the woman hurried away, Ronald appeared shaken for the first time. He began fumbling with the ties of his own life jacket. "Sir, I absolutely insist that you—"

He was interrupted by Tate and William, the steward, who ran up with the news that they had found a storage trunk filled with life jackets just down the deck. "Thank God," Ronald muttered, as he followed the others to the stash.

"Men,"Vanderbilt said as he saw the life jackets, "bring me all the kiddies you can find!"

Ronald shoved a jacket into Alfred's hand before running off. "Sir . . . I beg you," he said, looking him straight in the eye.

"Go, Ronald," was his reply.

The *Lusitania* rolled from a starboard list to her port side at 2:24, dragging the two remaining port lifeboats underwater. They had still been attached to the ship and filled with people.

Alfred was hurriedly fastening children into life jackets. Then, two at a time, one under each arm, he would run the children to the rail and hand them to anyone he could find who was also in a life jacket and composed enough to care for the child. Again and again, as fast as he could,Vanderbilt fought his way through the escalating chaos until there were no more children left to help. And he had run out of children at the same time he ran out of life jackets. The last jacket was tied to him.

Helen Smith, age six, was behind a deck chair, holding

tightly to an overturned potted plant when Ronald found
her at 2:25. Sobbing and cold, she told him her name and
begged him to "find Daddy and Mama." Gently, he picked
her up and carried her to Vanderbilt. "Sir, this is Helen. She
has lost her parents."

"Now then, sweetheart," he said soothingly as he quickly
removed his life jacket and fastened it onto the little girl.
"I'm sure your parents are in a boat looking for you right
now. Won't they be excited to see you float by?!"

He picked her up and carried her to a gentleman standing beside the rail. The water was over the man's shoes
and he appeared ready to enter the water. "Excuse me,"
Vanderbilt said. "This is Helen. She needs a friend with
whom to float while she waits on her mother and father.
Do you mind?" The man took her in his arms, managing a
smile for the child. "Thank you," Vanderbilt said and turned
back toward Ronald who stood beside the empty life jacket
trunk. It was 2:26.

"Have we lost William?" Ronald asked as Vanderbilt
approached.

"I put him aboard a lifeboat," Vanderbilt answered. "Had
to make him go. He's sixteen. Tate's gone. Swept over, but
in a jacket." Ronald nodded. For a brief moment, both
men stood side by side, almost at attention, detached somehow, completely calm, watching a nightmare unfold in
front of them, yet saying nothing.

Suddenly, Vanderbilt laughed ruefully. "All the houses I
owned around the world . . . most of them had swimming
pools. Curious, isn't it, considering this . . . that I never
learned to swim?"

"Sir, two times, you gave your own life jacket away. I
don't understand."

"Yes, you do, Ronald. You understand quite well. You aren't wearing a life jacket either. We made a choice, you and I. I have lived my life in luxury—sometimes in selfish luxury. But my children will be proud of me today. Our children will be proud of us.

"We changed the world's course in the past few minutes. We used our time to send children back to the living. They will now make a difference because of you. Their deeds will be a part of *your* legacy. The world has just now been set onto a better path, Ronald. And that path will echo through generations because of your actions today."

The valet reached over to shake Vanderbilt's hand but embraced him instead. "Thank you, sir."

"Thank you, my friend. It has been an honor and a pleasure. Now, if you don't mind, I have a trip to take." Vanderbilt smiled and began to walk away.

Suddenly, a thought struck him and Ronald called out. "Sir!" Vanderbilt turned. "Sir, we saved them . . . like the words on the medallion said."

Vanderbilt considered the idea briefly, then broke into a broad grin. "So we did," he said. "So we did."

As the men parted, each perhaps sensing a need to spend their last moments alone, the great ship groaned. It was the last cry of a dying beast, no longer able to muster the strength to fight. She rotated slowly until she lay on her starboard side. Then, bow first, as if anxious to flee the screams and prayers of the frantic surface, she slipped quickly into the quiet depths. The *Lusitania* disappeared at 2:28.

❧ Sixteen

Denver, Colorado—November

Dorry was in traffic when her cell phone rang. She saw on the caller ID that it was Mark and touched the button to connect.

He spoke immediately. "We found them. I'm at the station."

"Found what?"

"Who," Mark corrected. "We found the kids, the case I've been on . . . the ones I went to Memphis about? And they're alive."

"Oh, thank God," Dorry said. "What—where—I don't know what to ask."

"I don't have time now anyway. I just wanted to tell you the good news. I'll give you the whole scoop when I get home. I might be later than I'd planned. Remember, Abby and Dylan are coming over tonight."

"I remember." Dorry glanced at her watch. "Try not to be too late. Abby has left three messages on my cell—she's so excited—they have more news about the relics."

forced into a car. The woman who recognized them followed in *her* car and used her cell to phone it in. She stayed on them, relaying locations, right up until the Chicago guys took 'em down."

Abby said, "Wow. By your hand, the people shall be free. Had you thought of that?"

Mark nodded. "I've thought of a lot of things lately. *Especially* 'by your hand.'" He turned to Dorry. "Just so you know, I might be suspended."

"Why?" she asked incredulously. "For what?!"

"The captain told me no. Budget cuts, manpower shortages, changes in case jurisdiction, blah, blah, blah. I did it anyway. I just kept thinking about those kids out there somewhere . . . their parents dying a slow death . . . 'by *my* hand,' you know? I couldn't shake the thought that I had gotten these ideas from somewhere . . . God maybe . . ." Mark paused to see if they would laugh. They didn't. "And I couldn't get away from *by my hand!* Like, 'okay, you have the idea, but unless you *do* something . . .'" He sighed. "So I did."

Gently touching Mark's arm, Dorry asked, "You feel as though you did the right thing, don't you?"

He looked her in the eye. "Yes."

"So do I." Dylan and Abby were nodding too. "I would've wanted someone to do something if it had been Michael." Dorry shook her head as if to erase the thought. "Mark, we don't know. It might have been 'by your hand, the people shall *live.*' You may have saved their lives."

He stared at them for a moment, then said, "I thought of that before I did it. That's part of *why* I did it. I'm telling you guys, I don't mean to be melodramatic or anything, but these relics have changed me. This whole experience . . ."

"I'll be there as fast as I can. The kids were found in Chicago, by the way, so there's not much I have to do here until we get them home. I have their parents on the way there and Chicago PD is handling it on that end. So, I'll see you a little later. I sure do love you."

"Love you too," Dorry said, disconnecting the call. She was anxious to see Mark, but intended to call Michael immediately. As much as she missed him, Dorry was the tiniest bit sorry she'd agreed for him to stay an extra night with her parents.

Three days before, she had been unexpectedly sent out of town on assignment. That was only two days after she and Mark had last met with Dylan and Abby. Arrangements for Michael were never a problem when she had to travel for the *Post.* Usually, he just remained with Mark, but the boy also loved visiting his grandparents and, this time, had begged everyone to let him stay "a lot of days" with Papaw and Nana. Of course, Dorry's parents were delighted and insisted upon including an extra day to the three already scheduled. "This way," her mother had winked, "when you return, you and Mark can have an evening alone."

That "evening alone" had been postponed when Abby had called everyone together. She had gotten immediate and, according to her, amazing results from her friend in Wisconsin.

At seven o'clock on the dot, Dylan rang the doorbell. Dorry laughed as she welcomed them in. "I can set my watch by you two!"

"By one of us anyway. We've been standing on your doorstep for an hour," Abby exaggerated. They both wore their usual jeans and sweatshirts. Abby had a red backpack slung over one shoulder. "Dylan wouldn't ring your bell until *exactly* seven . . . o' . . . clock. He was looking at the second hand on his watch when he pushed the button."

Dylan put on his best holier-than-thou expression and announced, "*Early* is no more on time than *late. On time is on time.*"

"You are so strange," Abby said.

"That's why you love me," Dylan smirked and walked into the kitchen. "Hey, tacos again! We didn't even eat the last time we were here. I was hoping you'd saved those tacos. They are the same ones, aren't they?"

"No, smart guy, they're not," Dorry said.

"Well, I want 'em anyway."

"Help yourself." Then she said to Abby, "You're right, he *is* strange."

Mark wasn't as late as he had feared and came in while everyone else was seated around the kitchen table, just starting to eat. "Take off your tie and tell us about the kids," Dylan said. "Dorry filled us in. Congratulations."

"Yeah, thanks," he said and gave Dorry a "hello" kiss. "Give me about five seconds to eat two or three tacos and we'll talk. You guys hurry up and finish too."

After they had eaten, Dylan and Abby cleared the table while Dorry poured coffee. Mark began to talk. "Two children, a brother and sister. They were eight and ten when they disappeared from their front yard a year ago. Those ages are tough for us to determine what might have occurred—old enough that they could have run away and survived, yet young enough to be easily controlled or taken by someone—which is what happened."

"Who took them?" Dorry asked.

"It was a couple, and they did it with a knife. That's really all I know. They're sorting it all out in Chicago. I do

know this though"—Mark looked at Abby—"you helped get them back."

She looked shocked. "*I* helped! How did I help?"

"The last time we all met," Mark began, "you talked about the guy in Wisconsin . . ."

"Perry," she prompted.

"Yeah. You talked about him doing an age regression on the relics." She nodded. "After you guys left, that bothered me all night. Then it hit me: We needed to do an age *progression* on the kids—the opposite process. It's not usually done until someone has been missing for years, but I went in the next day, argued my point with the captain, and did it."

"What *was* your point?" Dylan asked.

"The changes shown by computer age progressions are not normally distinct after only a year. My argument was that while that might be true for a teenager, when a child is eight or ten, the changes in appearance after only a year can sometimes be drastic. Add that to whatever someone might do to further alter their looks . . ." He shrugged.

"Anyway, I did the workup with our computer people. We built a composite of fifteen pictures for each child. Different clothes, haircuts, hair colors, hats, the works."

"Mark," Dorry said, astounded. "You did this the day left? What was that, three days ago? How did all this happen so fast?"

"Michael was at your parents. You were gone. This is first I've been home. I stayed at the station and, during time, got some guys to help. We sent e-mails all day and night, with the composites, to eight hundred newspap and over a hundred television stations. We were still se ing them out when Chicago got the call. The kids v spotted being taken out of an apartment building

He closed his eyes, searching for the right words. Then, clarifying his thought, he said, "I don't mean that the objects themselves have changed me, but their message has changed my thinking . . . profoundly."

"How do *you* mean?" Abby asked.

"I'm starting to believe that I have spent my entire life playing defense, reacting to whatever happens instead of making things happen. Look at the people on our 'relic list.'" Mark gestured with both hands. "George Washington Carver *made* things happen. John Adams and Jonas Salk *made* things happen. Yeah, they all had ideas or a cause or whatever, but we remember them—the world changed— because of the action they took! Joan of Arc, William Wallace, Oskar Schindler—these people played offense!"

Dylan reached down by his chair for a manila folder. Opening it, he removed several pages and scattered them on the table, spreading them out with his hand. "Well," he said, "here are some more."

They were the same type of computer-generated pictures they had all seen before. Each exhibited the image of a statue, a painting, or a photograph, and in each, one of the relics was visible as well. On the top of each page, someone—Perasi, Mark assumed—had written a name in thick, black marker. They stared at the reproductions as if afraid to touch them, as though a line, somehow, had now been crossed.

"How many?" Mark asked, indicating the pages with a motion of his head.

"Eight," Dylan answered. "And they're still coming in."

Dorry picked up a picture of Queen Elizabeth I and moved some of the others around. "The good queen," she murmured. Then, to herself as much as anyone, she said,

"Her reign is still called the Elizabethan period. Art . . . discovery . . . everything flourished in England while she was on the throne."

Abby and Dylan had already seen them, of course, but Mark just sat, exhausted, staring at the pages. "I'm not even surprised, anymore, by who these people are," he said. "Don't get me wrong, I'm excited—thrilled even—but not surprised. It's as if these great people—maybe *all* the world's great people—have a secret that I *almost* understand. *Almost*, but not quite."

"I feel the same way," Dorry said. "As if some great revelation is hovering just beyond my reach."

Abby placed her backpack on the table. "I want to show you something. Would you get me a hand towel, please?" she asked. To one side, she set a UPS Overnight mailer, and to the other, a plain white envelope. And in the center of the table, as Dorry spread the towel, Abby carefully arranged the three artifacts. The Adams relic was positioned in the middle, Michael's object, *Live,* was to its left, and Mae Mae's food stone on the right.

They were strangely quiet. It was the first time Mark and Dorry had seen all three of the objects together. Indeed, it was the first time they had seen the Adams relic—*Free*—at all. It was slightly different from the other two, Dorry noticed, as if flayed open, somehow, on one side.

Abby began. "First of all, let me tell you that after the objects were regressed, it was obvious that they fit together perfectly. So there's the answer to one question," she said to Mark. "Yes, they belong together."

She continued. "I have, on paper, 3-D computer models of the regressed pieces. I also have a computer-generated picture of the object as it once was." She held up a page from the envelope, keeping its image turned toward her. "But I want you guys to discover it like I did. Mark, get behind Dorry so you can both view this at the same angle."

As Mark got up and moved to stand behind his wife, Abby slid the towel holding the objects toward them until they lined up vertically. The food stone was at the top, Michael's object at the bottom, with Adams' relic still in the middle.

"Okay," Mark said. "They are stacked—top to bottom— *Fed, Free,* and *Live.*"

"Right. That's what Dylan first noticed when I showed this to him. But to be honest, I'm not sure there is any importance in the order of the words. So stop thinking like an investigator. Think like an artist. View the object as a whole."

The Chandlers concentrated intently. Finally, Dorry said, "Talk to me, Ab."

"Okay. The edges need to fit. Remember the objects were misshapen by catastrophic pressure. Undo that damage in your mind's eye."

Abby and Dylan exchanged a glance as their friends focused, eyes narrowed and steady, determined to see through the objects in front of them and into the past. Mark stood with his arms folded, occasionally bringing a hand to his chin. Dorry rested her fingertips on the edge of the table. Her head was cocked slightly to the right when, carefully, never shifting her gaze from the relics, she sat up a little straighter. "Abby," she said, "can I move them?"

"Yes."

Deliberately, Dorry reached for the relic that had belonged to John Adams. It was the one in the middle. Pausing only for a second, she moved it to the top, its flayed, slightly open side, pointing up. Dorry picked up the food stone next. With its one edge closed by pressure, she placed it at the bottom where its other side, the rounded edge, faced down. And last, Dorry saw, with both of its edges closed, the object her son had discovered, fit neatly into the middle position.

Holding her breath, Abby asked quietly, "What do you see, Dorry?"

Dorry reached out and brushed her palm across the objects, tenderly touching all three at the same time. She looked at her husband and said, "It's a cup."

For a moment, time itself seemed to stand still. No one said anything or moved. Suddenly unsure he could remain standing, Mark went back to his chair and sat down heavily. "It's a cup," Dorry said again. "Do you see it?" she asked Mark, who nodded numbly.

Abby placed the computer-generated picture on the table. With its edges regressed, the closures undone, and the pieces placed together, it was indeed the perfect image of a cup. The computer had even defined the object's original color, and the vivid, coppery-gold glint of its reflection smoldered from the page.

Abby pointed to the bottom of the cup in the picture. It existed on the page as a rounded curve. "See what's missing?" She picked up the food stone and turned it over. "Remember? We said it was as if something was attached here at one time? It was the base."

"So there *is* one more piece," Dorry said as a fact. "We are missing the cup's base."

"Without a doubt," Abby replied. She looked at the picture and turned the food stone over in her hand a few times before replacing it in its position on the table. "It—

the base, wherever it is—would be round . . . and flat." She thought for a minute. "There is not a stem. Cups of that period were either flat-bottomed or melted directly onto a precast base." Having already noted the round bottom of the cup, Abby reached over and tapped the small, dime-sized spot on the food stone. "This cup had a base."

"So we aren't missing a stem," Dylan said. "Meaning, we aren't lacking two more pieces."

"One piece," Abby stated definitively.

"What about the writing?" Mark asked. "Would there be script on the base?"

"Probably," Abby responded. "Another message perhaps, maybe something that explains the script on the body of the cup. It might even have the mark, or seal, of the maker."

Mark gestured with his head to the side of the table indicating the pictures, now neatly stacked, of the men and women whose actions had changed the world in which he lived. "I wonder . . . are they so different from us? What did they know that we don't know?"

No one else spoke.

Slowly, Mark reached out both hands. With infinite care, he surrounded the objects with his palms and picked up all three at once. Holding them toward his wife and friends, he asked, "After all this time . . . why has this come together now? Where is the last piece? What happens if we find it? Do we understand more about our purpose? Or every-thing? Is there a message in that last piece that will change me somehow? Or will it change the world?"

Mark whispered, "What am I missing here?"

⭐ SEVENTEEN

NEW YORK CITY—JUNE 11, 1915

THE BOYS PLAYED ON THE FLOOR AT HER FEET AS Margaret Vanderbilt held an envelope in her hands and stared out the open parlor window of the mansion. It was a beautiful afternoon, clear and warm. She watched as a stable boy curried the Appaloosa—a gift from Alfred on their last wedding anniversary. Margaret loved the animal, but absently wondered if she would ever ride again. The passion for horses she had shared with her husband, she feared, had surely died with him.

For a week after his death, Margaret never left her hotel room, but friends had finally persuaded her to move back into their home on Fifty-seventh Street. There, the staff kept reporters at bay as the young widow grieved. She was in agony, unable to eat or think or accomplish anything beyond the barest care for the two boys, Alfred Jr. and George, who were too young to understand what had happened.

Alfred's body had never been recovered. For a time, Margaret held out hope that he had been rescued by a passing fishing boat and perhaps taken to a remote village on the Irish coast, unconscious and unable to get word to her, but as the days passed, she resigned herself to the obvious truth—her husband was gone forever.

Newspapers were full of stories from survivors about the horrible last moments of the tragedy. Margaret forced herself to read every one and as the eyewitness accounts of Alfred's gallant actions that day began to come to light, she cut those articles out to save for the boys. It was a small consolation now, but as little Alfred and George grew up, she felt, it would be important for them to know that their heritage was one of character and courage. Their father had died a hero.

Margaret shifted in the chair and smoothed the front of her dark blue dress with her hands. Crossing her legs, she wiped a tear from her cheek with a handkerchief and read the letter again. It had arrived by special courier from the post office earlier that morning, and she had almost fainted when she saw the handwriting. It was addressed to "The Young Masters Vanderbilt" in care of her. Posted from Liverpool on May 22, it was one of several hundred letters recovered from a floating mailbag and forwarded by Cunard only two weeks after the disaster. Margaret's brief hope for good news was dashed as she opened the envelope and saw that it had been written by her husband on May 6, the day before the sinking.

Inside the envelope, wrapped around a much longer letter to Alfred Jr. and George, was a personal note to her. Written in his familiar flowing script, it read:

Darling,

I send you my love across the miles. It is early evening and I am on deck, alone with my thoughts of you and our precious little ones.

Anxious though I may be to share everything this instant, my own thoughts and emotions are jumbled to such a state that I must
beg your patience. Suffice to say that a great
revelation has now come into our lives. An
object—an antiquity, if you will—has opened
corners in my mind and heart that I scarcely
knew existed.

The boys are young and will not understand, but somehow I feel it important that
you read the enclosed letter to them now.
Save it, of course, and I shall explain all upon
my return.

My prayer, as always, is for your safety while
we are apart and that you might feel my arms
around you as though I'd never left.

Your adoring husband,
Alfred

Margaret sobbed as she held the note to her breast.
She had been certain that there were no more tears to
cry, but every day brought a new memory, a smell, or
some tangible reminder of the man she had loved more
than her own life. She was not sure she wanted to live
without him. *Were it not for the boys* . . . she mused . . .
and then, quickly banished the evil thought from her
mind.

Shaking her head, Margaret drew a deep breath and
wiped her eyes. Alfred had departed this earth having left
behind more questions than answers. An antiquity? A

great revelation in *our* lives? And how might an object open corners in one's mind and heart, she wondered.

Margaret had already read the letter meant for the boys several times to herself, and while beautiful and eloquent, it only added to her confusion. In it, however, Alfred had referred to "words" that had changed his life. Did these "words" have something to do with the object about which he had written? He had not said, but she noted with awe that she was strangely comforted by their presence in the letter.

The "words" were written in the form of a memorandum, and while Margaret knew they had been meant for the boys, she determined to copy them down for herself. She would read them over and over again, as Albert had instructed his children to do. *Might there be,* she thought, *a corner in my own mind and heart that can be opened?*

She gazed up at the parlor's chandelier, spreading gracefully from the fourteen-foot ceiling. Closing her eyes, Margaret prayed for strength and hope, wisdom and courage. Then, to her husband, she promised to bring up their children as he would have wished. She told him that she would not be bitter about his physical absence in their lives. Rather, she would be grateful for the years they had lived and loved and laughed with each other. And she told him good-bye.

When Margaret opened her eyes, she found Alfred Jr. and George standing quietly beside her. George had placed his tiny hand on her knee. Smiling for the first time in a month, she scooped George onto her lap and kissed his face. With her left arm, she drew little Alfred close and kissed him too. Then, Margaret unfolded the letter to the boys and read it aloud.

My dear, sweet Ones,

My first thought upon rising this morning
was of you, and my heart is full to the bursting. You may be surprised to hear that my last
thought of the evening before was also of you.
My voyage on this great ship has been slow
and uneventful, and I miss your laughter and
antics tremendously. The time alone, however,
has given me occasion for reflection not often
enjoyed under normal circumstances.

Never given to undue emotion, I have lately
been overwhelmed with a feeling of love and
responsibility for your future that drives me to
tears. I feel somehow compelled to write down
and send a specific message I have received for
you. It was my intention to read the words to
you in person, but time, I fear, is of the essence.

You are very young and will not understand
these thoughts at this moment. No matter.
They will be read to you for now. When you
are older, you will read them yourself again
and again. Then, again and again. Only when
their meaning is imprinted in your heart will
you realize their power and *your* purpose.

These ancient words, translated from an
object in my possession, have most recently
changed my life. Let them now direct yours.
One day, when I am gone, the world will most
likely babble on about the money you will
have inherited. But more than anything, I
want you to understand that the message of

the following words are the most valuable legacy with which one could ever be provided. Here now is your true inheritance—the gift from a father to his son.

I made you different from the others.

On the planet Earth, there has never been one like you . . . and there never will be again.

Your spirit, your thoughts and feelings, your ability to reason—all exist in no one else.

Your eyes are a masterpiece, incomparable, and windows to a soul that is also uniquely yours.

A single strand of your hair has been created especially for you. Of the multitudes who have come before you and the multitudes who may follow, not one of them duplicates the formula with which I made you.

I made you different from the others.

The blood that flows through your veins flows through the heart of one whom I have chosen. The rarities that make you one of a kind, my child, are no mere accident or quirk of fate.

I made you different in order that you might make a difference.

You have been created with the ability to change the world. Every single choice you make . . . every single action you take . . . matters. But remember, the converse is also true. Every choice you do not make . . . every action you do not take . . . matters just as much!

Your actions cannot be hoarded, saved for later, or used selectively. By your hand, millions of lives will be altered, caught up in a chain of events begun by you this very day. But the opposite is true as well. Millions of lives are also altered, caught up in an entirely different chain of events—if you choose to wait.

You possess the power of choice. Free will. You have been given everything you need to act, but the choice is yours alone. And beginning this very moment, you will choose wisely.

Now go. And never feel inadequate again. Do not dwell in thoughts of insignificance or wander aimlessly, lost, like a sheep.

You are powerful. You matter. And you have been found.

You are my choice.

Your Father

⚔ Epilogue

MARK AND DORRY LIVE IN THE SAME HOUSE ON Autumn Ridge Circle, though they are currently contemplating a larger residence. Michael, a third grader now, is a proud "big brother" to Tracy Elizabeth Chandler, the two-year-old sister who worships his every move.

Dorry resigned from the *Post* when she became pregnant with Tracy. While she hasn't yet won a Pulitzer, Dorry maintains a heavy schedule of freelance work that includes pieces for *Atlantic Monthly* and *Newsweek,* as well as an occasional article for *USA Today.*

At forty-one years of age, Mark Chandler became the youngest chief of police in Denver's history. By the time city fathers made the appointment, Mark had already received four commendations from different states recognizing his part in saving the lives of missing children. The first commendation was awarded by Colorado's own governor for Mark's actions in rescuing the brother and sister he had located in Chicago, though at the time of the ceremony,

Mark was still on suspension for "disobeying the order of a superior officer."

Abby and Dylan have become the Chandlers' babysitters of choice. They announced their engagement to be married last spring and now consider the time with Michael and Tracy to be "practice." While Dylan remains in his position at the Denver Museum, Abby went back to school and is now finishing her doctoral program in archaeological chemistry.

The couples have become best friends, meeting for lunch regularly or for dinner and a movie. When together, they often discuss the mystery that brought them into each other's lives. Before the Adams' piece was returned to the Smithsonian, Abby created a ceramic cast of the object. Often, the four friends will lay the reproduction out with the other two relics and theorize about the missing base.

They talk of the proof they've already uncovered that one person, by his or her own hand, can change the world. They discuss the changes in their own lives—their missions, their life's purpose—brought about by the simple lessons inscribed on the three relics. Yet, there is always an undercurrent of frustration—evidence of the many questions remaining unanswered.

Mark, Dorry, Abby, and Dylan have come to their own individual, unshakable convictions about the origin of the cup. And to a person, they believe that the base of the cup, when it is found and understood, will provide hope, and a specific message, to a world of people seeking answers of their own.

The *Lusitania* still rests at the bottom of the Irish Sea. Eleven-and-one-half miles off the green cliffs of Brow Head in County Cork, near the town of Cobh, the once-grand ocean liner lays on her starboard side beneath 312 feet of water. Vast schools of fish circle the vessel, using the same routes over and over again, as if to guard the memories buried there. Her bow thrusts upward at a forty-five-degree angle, the outline of her name still visible.

The seabed is littered with broken plates, bowls, and large chunks of coal. The ship's triple-toned whistle rests by itself on the sea floor, near the crumbled and collapsing bridge, while a bathtub sits upright near the stern. The pipe and showerhead rise above it, still attached, as if waiting to be used.

Sadly, however, it appears as though the last piece of the puzzle—the medallion, the cup's base—might never be recovered. The object still remains inside the jewel box. No longer purple, the expensive material that gave the box its color has long since decayed. The case is exactly where it was left so many years ago, resting in the upper left-hand corner of the closet, nestled against the wall in an ever-increasing blanket of sediment. Regal B-65 and 67, a starboard-side suite, is now, due to the wreck's position, at the very bottom of tons of disintegrating steel.

The *Lusitania* is collapsing in on herself. Time and the ocean's relentless pressure have done more damage than Schwieger's torpedo. Unexploded depth charges, the remaining vestige of an Irish naval exercise in the 1940s, are scattered all over the wreck. They are extremely dangerous and, coupled with the fragile condition of the structure itself, make any exploration of the ship's interior virtually impossible.

The life of Alfred Vanderbilt has continued to be a source of speculation throughout the decades as inquisitive historians and proud descendants seek to make sense of his extraordinary final act. Thousands of articles in newspapers and magazines all over the world have been written about his courage that day. And each printed story has been clipped and meticulously filed in a private vault in the western United States. There, a records repository of the Vanderbilt family is maintained that begins with the first journal notes of Alfred Vanderbilt's great-grandfather, Cornelius, as a young man in 1832. Established before Cornelius' death, this is the collection of a family whose sense of its own history is proud and complete.

With monthly entries submitted over the lifetimes of what are now more than one hundred descendants of Cornelius and begun before the advent of modern record keeping, the files are vast and physically enormous. The vault includes every conceivable particle of each family member's life, from financial records, personal notes, invitations, and newspaper articles to birthday cards, grocery lists, and receipts from the veterinarian. Insisted upon by the patriarch of the Vanderbilt family and intended as a preventive measure against the possibility of frivolous lawsuits, it also serves as an incredibly comprehensive family history.

And so, there is still hope that the power of the message inscribed so carefully on the base of the cup will one day be revealed to the world. In a wooden cabinet on the sixth row, indistinguishable among the racks of identical cabinets lining the huge vault, the second drawer from the top holds an envelope whose paper is stained with seawater. It was submitted to be filed in the Vanderbilt family repository on April 25, 1927, by Alfred's youngest son, George, and has never been removed.

The only existing translation of the relic is labeled PYA42563. And just like the other three pieces of the cup, it is hiding in plain sight.

The farther backward you can look, the farther forward you are likely to see.

—Winston Churchill

❧ About the Author

ANDY ANDREWS is a best-selling novelist and speaker whose combined works have been translated into nearly twenty languages and have sold millions of copies worldwide. *The Traveler's Gift,* a featured book selection of ABC's *Good Morning America,* was on the *New York Times* bestseller list for seventeen weeks. As a speaker and corporate entertainer for the world's largest organizations, he is in constant demand. Andy has spoken at the request of four different United States presidents and toured military bases around the world, speaking to troops at the request of the United States Department of Defense. Arguably, there is no single person on the planet better at weaving subtle, yet life-changing lessons into riveting tales of adventure and intrigue—both on paper and on stage.

Find out more about a man one *New York Times* writer called "a modern-day Will Rogers who has quietly become one of the most influential people in America" at www.AndyAndrews.com.

⚜ ACKNOWLEDGMENTS

IN AN UNDERTAKING OF THIS SORT, THE LIST OF people to whom gratitude is owed can be overwhelming. I am blessed to be surrounded by friends and family who have become a team of which I am thrilled to be a part. If one perceives me as a person who makes good and informed choices, it is only because of my reliance on the counsel of these people.

Thank you all for your presence in my life.

. . . to Polly, my wife, who has read endless drafts, participated in many "what if" conversations, and has endured occasional blank stares at dinnertime as I was lost somewhere in Tuskegee or on the *Lusitania*. I love you and our life together.

. . . to Robert D. Smith, my personal manager and champion who never, ever loses faith. The smartest business person I know, you are also one of the few people of whom I am aware that everyone loves. This, my friend, is a tough combination to beat.

. . . to Gail and Mike Hyatt. Your belief in Robert, me, and our work started it all. Thanks for your friendship and example.

. . . to Jenny Baumgartner, my editor at Thomas Nelson. This book would not have been the same without you. The last chapter particularly benefited from your input.

. . . to Jonathan Merkh, Jerry Park, and Pamela Clements. Your encouragement means more than you will ever know.

. . . to Todd Rainsberger, whose idea became the title of this book. Thanks also for helping me shape the story line. Your influence on *The Lost Choice* was invaluable . . . almost as important as your influence in my life.

. . . to Kevin Perkins, my wise and calm friend. With a laugh and a few words, you can always talk me off the ledge!

. . . to Maryann and Dave Winck—the neighbors and friends of a lifetime. Our boys love you, we love you, and everyone knows that nothing would work at our house if it weren't for you, Dave!

. . . to Foncie and Joe Bullard, whose friendship, courage, belief, and example are a constant inspiration to me. Thanks also for the use of your beach house so that I can continue to write when my own is too loud!

. . . to Mike Jakubik who makes me laugh, Don Brindley who makes me think, and Katrina and Jerry Anderson who are always on my side no matter what. Thanks for your presence in my life and the lives of my family.

. . . to Sandy Stimpson, Barbara Selvey, Gloria and Martin Gonzalez, Maryann and Jerry Tyler, Sunny Brownlee, Richard Stimpson, Brent Burns, Kathy and Dick Rollins, and Patsy Jones. Your influence in my life is undeniable and very much appreciated.

. . . to Zachary Smith, my webmaster and all around

smartest person on the planet. Your eye for detail, playful spirit, and patience with my computer illiteracy is appreciated.

. . . to Ron Land, Dave Shepard, Darlene Quinn, Danielle Douglas, and Blythe McIntosh at Thomas Nelson. Your skills and energy always amaze me.

Special thanks to Scott Jeffrey, the man who coaches me and improves everything I do. You are making my "Impossible Journeys" very possible indeed.

And finally, to Austin and Adam, my little boys. You are the very beating of my heart. Nothing compares to the feeling I get when you guys run into my arms as I walk through the door. I love you.

⚹ BIBLIOGRAPHY

Author's Note: Extensive research was conducted to carefully determine dates, exact times, and other details. Any historical errors that might have slipped through my finely meshed "net of accuracy" are entirely my own; however, what the reader may occasionally determine to be a mistake is most likely the product of contradictory source information. In such instances, the author simply selected the most reasonable fact from among the many choices.

Birds of North America. Washington, D.C.: National Geographic Society, 1999.

Blum, Howard. *The Gold of Exodus*. New York: Simon & Schuster, 1998.

Brecher, Elinor. *Schindler's Legacy—True Stories of the List Survivors*. New York: The Penguin Group, 1994.

Brown, Dan. *Deception Point*. New York: Simon & Schuster, 2001.

Collins, Gail. *America's Women*. New York: HarperCollins Publishers, 2003.

Collins, Max Allan. *The Lusitania Murders*. New York: Berkley Publishing Group, 2002.

Duncan, Todd. *Life by Design*. Nashville: J. Countryman, 2002.

Ellis, Joseph J. *Founding Brothers*. New York: Random House, 2000.

Ford, Emma. *Falconry: The Art and Practice*. Blandford Press, 1992.

Hickey, Des, and Gus Smith. *Seven Days to Disaster*. London: William Collins Sons and Co., 1981.

Keneally, Thomas. *Schindler's List*. New York: Scribner, 1982.

Kerrigan, Michael. *What Choice Do I Have?* Possibility Press, 2002.

Lansky, Bruce. *35,000 Baby Names*. New York: Meadowbrook Press, 1995.

Lewis, Bernard. *Race and Slavery in the Middle East*. Oxford: Oxford University Press, 1990.

Mason, John. *Conquering an Enemy Called Average*. Tulsa: Insight International, 1996.

McCullough, David. *John Adams*. New York: Touchstone, 2001.

Preston, Diana. *Lusitania . . . An Epic Tragedy*. New York: Berkley Publishing Group, 2002.

Simpson, Colin. *The Lusitania*. Boston: Little, Brown and Company, 1972.

Steinhouse, Herbert. "The Real Oskar Schindler." New York: *Saturday Night Magazine*, April 1994.

TIME Special Issue. New York: Time, Inc., July 7, 2003.

❧ INTERNET REFERENCE SOURCES

abacci.com

Africawithin.com

Aggie-horticulture.tamu.edu

ai.MIT.edu

AmericanPresidents.org

amnh.org

angelfire.com

AttitudePump.com

Auburn.edu

bartleby.com

bibarch.com

brinkster.com

business.com

ByFaithOnly.com

byteNet.net

campsilos.org

campus.northpark.edu

center4sinai.com

CGHS.Dade.com

CityVibz.com

civilization.CA.edu

cmp.CalTech.edu

college.hmco.com

colonialhall.com

cs.Indiana.edu

Denver.org

DenverPost.com

DMNH.org

EarlyAmerica.com

EasyFunSchool.com

econedlink.org

english.UPenn.edu

etext.lib.Virginia.edu

FindaGrave.com

fortunecity.com

flatirons.org

flownet.com

fwkc.com

galegroup.com

GaTech.edu

geocities.com

GlobalSecurity.org

gospelcom.net

gwu.edu

harcourtschool.com

heritageharbor.org

highlanderweb.co.uk

history.org

HomeofHeros.com
hoover.archives.gov
hpol.org
ibis.com
invent.org
inventors.about.com
IPL.org
JoeBullard.com
JohnstonArchive.net
KU.edu
Law.Cornell.edu
Law.UMKC.edu
LearningFamily.net
lib.IAState.edu
LostLiners.org
luminet.net
Lusitania.net
lybot.com
memory.loc.gov
multied.com
myhero.com
myriobiblos.com
nanosft.com
NPS.gov
odur.net
OskarSchindler.com
OSPAC.org
100megsfree4.com
Patterson-UNCF.org
PBS.org
petragrail.tripod.com
press-pubs.uchicago.edu
Princeton.edu
probertencyclopedia.com
remember.org

RooseveltPresidency.ucsb.edu
rumkatkilise.org
quotationspage.com
SemRedCross.org
sivir.com
sjcs-history.org
solohq.com
StephenHopkins.com
telemanage.CA
Templeresearch.eclipse.com
TheTrueEntrepreneur.com
TheTruthSeeker.co.UK
thinkquest.org
topicsite.com
Tulane.edu
tumasekusa.com
UGA.com
UShistory.org
US-Israel.org
UVA.org
VictorySeeds.gov
vision.org (Richard Pilant)
wallbuilders.com
WhatsTheNumber.com
Whitehouse.gov
Wikipedia.org
Wildmanstevebrill.com
WISC.edu
WPI.edu
wringtonsomerset.org
WVhumanities.org

CORPORATE PRESENTATIONS

Invite Andy to speak to your organization and your audience members will never be the same again. Andy brings new insights to dealing with problems, outlining the essential steps necessary for greater individual fulfillment and increasing corporate profitability. He'll explain how to eliminate mental safety nets that keep us from reaching our goals. Plus, Andy will share the life-changing principles found in his international best-seller, *The Traveler's Gift*, tailoring the presentation to your organization's needs.

CONTACT ANDY

Book Andy for your corporate event:
(800) 726-ANDY (2639)

Learn more at
www.AndyAndrews.com

OTHER PRODUCTS BY ANDY

TIMELESS WISDOM FROM THE TRAVELER
(8 CDs and Guidebook)
An in-depth analysis of the profound lessons revealed in Andy's modern classic, *The Traveler's Gift*.

MY LIFE SO FAR: AN EVENING WITH ANDY ANDREWS (CD)
In this rare live recording, this master storyteller takes you on an incredible journey through the fascinating, funny, and inspiring tales of his life so far.

NOT NORMAL: THE POWER TO BE DIFFERENT (DVD)
Features Andy live in concert presenting over eighty-minutes of hilarious, emotionally-charged tales.

THE TRAVELER'S GIFT
Seven Decisions That Determine Personal Success

"The Traveler's Gift *touched me in a way no other book ever has."*
—BARBARA JOHNSON, Humorist and Best-selling Author of
Stick a Geranium in Your Hat and Be Happy

*"The type of advice that you've always needed to hear—but never took the time
to listen to. You'll gain wisdom in only a few hours from this book!"*
—TIM SANDERS, Chief Solutions Officer for Yahoo! and Author of
Love Is the Killer App: How to Win Business and Influence Friends

"The Traveler's Gift *provides a powerful and compelling road map through the
highways of life."*
—JOHN SCHUERHOLZ, General Manager, Atlanta Braves

David Ponder has lost his job and the will to live. When he is super-
naturally selected to travel through time, he visits historical figures such
as Abraham Lincoln, King Solomon, and Anne Frank. Each visit yields
a Decision for Success that will one day impact the entire world.

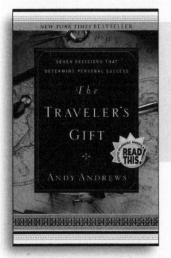

New York Times BEST-SELLER!

Good Morning America BOOK CLUB PICK!

Wall Street Journal BEST-SELLER!

USA Today BEST-SELLER!

Publishers Weekly BEST-SELLER!

ISBN: 0-7852-6428-0

Also available on audio
ISBN 0-7852-6138-9

ALSO AVAILABLE

THE TRAVELER'S GIFT JOURNAL

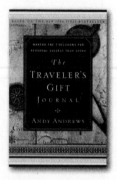

As the perfect companion to *The Traveler's Gift,* this journal gives you the opportunity to record your own experiences as you internalize these decisions—just as David did in his travels. Filled with quotes from the book and guided questions to direct readers, *The Traveler's Gift Journal* is a powerful tool for all who seek success.

ISBN: 1-4041-0131-4

THE YOUNG TRAVELER'S GIFT

In his senior year of high school, Michael hits rock bottom. Facing the bleak future ahead, he sees no way out and wonders if life is really worth living. But with some divine intervention, he's given a second chance when he's offered a once-in-a-lifetime journey of discovery.

Written to engage the minds of teens and tweens, *The Young Traveler's Gift* is sure to encourage and enlighten young men and women as they prepare to face the journeys that lie ahead.

ISBN: 1-4003-0427-X

ANDY ANDREWS'
The Lost Choice INITIATIVE

A single choice can transform your life, changing the world around you in ways you may never know. Grabbing hold of *The Lost Choice,* you make a firm commitment—an irrefutable decision leading to a cascade of unforeseen opportunities.

One way to solidify a major decision is to put it in writing. (Research has proven the effectiveness of this technique.) Another way is to proclaim your decision to another person—perhaps someone who will keep you accountable—or even to a group of people. THE LOST CHOICE INITIATIVE takes this idea one step further. Here, you have a forum for proclaiming your personal decision to the world!

There's no decision too big or too small: Will you do your part to end world hunger? Or achieve your ideal weight? Create world peace? Live with peace of mind? Contribute to your community? Schedule time alone for self-reflection and dreaming? Write a book? Spend more time with your kids? The possibilities are boundless . . .

Making a decision sets in motion a series of events beyond what we can comprehend in the physical world. With the choice in your hand, forces go to work to help you in your cause. And you're never alone. The purpose of this initiative is for people from all walks of life to come together and share their decisions. Collaborations, even if only at the level of thought, can help move us in the direction we are committed to moving.

After reading *The Lost Choice,* what is a major decision you are making from this day forth?

Engage your decision at
www.TheLostChoice.com